USN DESTROYER
vs
IJN DESTROYER

The Pacific 1943

MARK STILLE

First published in Great Britain in 2012 by Osprey Publishing,
Midland House, West Way, Botley, Oxford, OX2 0PH, UK
44-02 23rd Street, Suite 219, Long Island City, NY 11101, USA

E-mail: info@ospreypublishing.com

Osprey Publishing is part of the Osprey Group

A CIP catalog record for this book is available from the British Library

Print ISBN: 978 1 84908 623 3
PDF ebook ISBN: 978 1 84908 624 0
ePub ebook ISBN: 978 1 78200 319 9

Index by Sandra Shotter
Typeset in ITC Conduit and Adobe Garamond
Maps by Peter Bull Art Studio
Originated by PDQ Digital Media Solutions, Bungay, UK
Printed in China through Bookbuilders

12 13 14 15 16   10 9 8 7 6 5 4 3 2 1

Osprey Publishing is supporting the Woodland Trust, the UK's leading
woodland conservation charity, by funding the dedication of trees.

www.ospreypublishing.com

Author's acknowledgments

The author is indebted to Robert Hanshew from the Naval History and
Heritage Command Photographic Section, the Yamato Museum, and Tohru
Kizu, editor of *Ships of the World* magazine for their assistance in procuring the
photographs used in this title. Additionally, the author wishes to thank Keith
Allen and Commander Mike Lynch, USN, for their help in clarifying several
points.

Artist's note

Readers may care to note that the original painting from which the battlescene
of this book was prepared is available for private sale. All reproduction
copyright whatsoever is retained by the Publishers. All inquiries should be
addressed to:

Giuseppe Rava
via Borgotto 17
48018 Faenza (RA)
Italy

www.g-rava.it
info@g-rava.it

The Publishers regret that they can enter into no correspondence upon this
matter.

Editor's note

For ease of comparison please refer to the following conversion table:

1 mile = 1.6km
1yd = 0.9m
1ft = 0.3m
1in = 2.54cm/25.4mm
1 gallon (US) = 3.8 liters
1 ton (US) = 0.9 metric tons
1lb = 0.45kg

CONTENTS

INTRODUCTION

Entering the Pacific War, both the United States Navy and the Imperial Japanese Navy (IJN) possessed large numbers of destroyers. Each navy had a different idea of how it would employ its destroyers, but each expected them to play important roles. The Americans designed their destroyers to conduct a number of important missions. The most important of these were surface attack against major enemy fleet units and defense of the battle line from Japanese torpedo attack, but other missions included scouting and providing antiaircraft and antisubmarine screening for fleet operations. For its part, the IJN placed a great emphasis on developing large destroyers with a very heavy torpedo armament to enable them to play a critical role in reducing the strength of the American battle line in advance of the expected decisive clash between battle fleets. The Japanese also developed a powerful, long-range torpedo for their destroyers, which greatly increased their offensive potential.

The two destroyer forces played supporting roles in the first phase of the war. Following the surprise Japanese air attack on the American Pacific Fleet at Pearl Harbor, the Imperial Fleet began a relentless period of expansion. This came to a close in May 1942 at the battle of Coral Sea. The following month, when the Japanese attempted to regain offensive momentum in the Central Pacific, they were defeated at the battle of Midway. This battle greatly reduced the offensive power of the IJN, but it did not erase the IJN's superiority over the Pacific Fleet in every category, including destroyers.

Neither the Americans nor the Japanese considered that the site of the decisive clash between their two navies would be the Solomon Islands. Following the battle of Midway, the Americans were quicker to gain the initiative. On August 7, 1942 they launched an invasion of the southern Solomon Islands, landing at Guadalcanal and other points. This began a 16-month campaign for control of the Solomons that constituted the most sustained campaign of the Pacific War and the second-longest naval campaign of the war after the struggle for control of the Atlantic. During the Solomons campaign, a total of 14 significant battles were fought. Of these, two were carrier battles, two were major surface engagements involving battleships on one or both sides, another six were fought between mixed cruiser and destroyer forces, and four were fought solely between destroyers.

The first part of the Solomons campaign exhibited the prowess of the IJN on an individual unit basis, but also ended in defeat for the Japanese. During the battles around Guadalcanal from August until November 1942, the Japanese lost 18 naval ships, including 11 destroyers. The victorious Americans paid a heavier price of 25 ships, including 15 destroyers. In the end, the possession of the airfield on Guadalcanal dictated the winner, and the Japanese were never able to marshal sufficient forces to wrest control of the airfield from the Americans, or even to neutralize it except on a single, brief occasion. During the battle for Guadalcanal, Japanese destroyers played an important role since they were employed in a transport capacity to deliver supplies at night to the Japanese garrison on the island. The speed of the destroyers allowed them to approach the island, deliver troops and supplies, and leave the area – all during the hours of darkness thus avoiding air attack. On several

During the early part of the Solomons campaign, Japanese destroyermen had a field day against American commanders who did not appreciate the power of the Type 93 torpedo and failed to maneuver their forces accordingly. At the battle of Tassafaronga on November 30, four American cruisers were hit by torpedoes. *Minneapolis* is shown here in Tulagi harbor after the battle with her bow blown off. (NHHC 80-G-211215)

Sazanami, a Group II unit of the Special Type, is shown in this 1940 view. The increased size of the bridge structure over that of the Group I ships is evident, and the triple torpedo mounts have been provided with shields. *Sazanami* survived into 1944 and was sunk by an American submarine in January. (Yamato Museum)

occasions, they used their powerful torpedoes to inflict heavy losses on the US Navy during the vicious night battles fought around the island. American destroyers were continually used in a subsidiary role since American admirals were wedded to the big gun as the decisive element of naval warfare. This doctrine, and American torpedo quality, meant American destroyers played an insignificant role during the battle.

When the campaign shifted to the Central Solomons beginning in March 1943, the Japanese destroyer force was thrust into a leading role since the Japanese were increasingly reluctant to commit their heavy units to the grinding battle of attrition that the struggle for the Solomons had become. The Japanese destroyer force was losing its fine edge due to losses and heavy use, but as at Guadalcanal, destroyers were called on to reinforce (and on occasion withdraw) garrisons in the Central and Northern Solomons as well as keep them supplied.

The Americans still clung to the notion that big guns were the key to victory and built their night surface forces around cruisers. Since the Guadalcanal campaign had taken a heavy toll of the heavy cruiser force, and since faster-firing light cruisers were seen as more suitable for taking on Japanese destroyers, these were used as the centerpiece of American night-combat surface forces. At the battles of Kula Gulf and Kolombangara in July 1943, four Allied light cruisers were either sunk or damaged. At this point, the Americans decided that chasing Japanese destroyers with cruisers was a losing strategy. Concurrent with the heavy losses in cruisers and the realization that employing them in the constrained waters of the Solomons was excessively risky, the American destroyer force developed the tactics and the weapons to fight on its own. By August 1943, the American destroyers were freed from being solely screening units

for cruisers. More importantly, the defects in the American destroyer-launched torpedo had finally been identified and corrected. For the first time, American destroyers had a dependable weapon to employ against the Japanese. The combination of new tactics, reliable torpedoes, and the technological advantage provided by radar, gave American destroyers a winning edge.

The Japanese destroyer force entered the campaign with superior training, discipline, and weapons in the form of the long-range Type 93 torpedo. However, the Japanese started the war without radar, giving the Americans a huge technological advantage that had the potential to negate Japanese advantages in other areas. For the Japanese, the campaign in the Central and Northern Solomons cost them another 21 destroyers. The losses in both phases of the Solomons campaign gutted the finely trained and equipped Japanese destroyer force. The IJN's destroyers were not a significant factor for the remainder of the war.

Four of the last five surface battles of the campaign, all fought at night, were contested solely between destroyers. These four destroyer battles are the subject of this book. Two of the four were clear American victories, one was a tactical Japanese victory, and the last a draw.

A June 1942 view of Yugumo-class unit *Naganami*. The ship represented the epitome of Japanese destroyer design and presents a powerful, balanced appearance. (Yamato Museum)

CHRONOLOGY

1942

January 24

Four World War I "four-stacker" destroyers conduct the first American destroyer torpedo attack of the war, attacking a Japanese invasion convoy bound for Balikpapan in the Dutch East Indies. Firing old Mark 8 torpedoes using the reliable Mark 3 contact exploder, they sink three Japanese transports and damage two others at no loss to themselves.

February 27

The battle of the Java Sea. Of the 153 Japanese Type 93 torpedoes launched during the action, only three hit. However, these sank two Dutch cruisers and a destroyer, providing the measure of victory for the Japanese.

August 9

The battle of Savo Island, the first naval clash of the Solomons campaign. The Japanese sink four Allied heavy cruisers and damage a fifth with gunfire and torpedoes. Only one American destroyer even employs its torpedoes, and it misses.

October 11–12

The battle of Cape Esperance. In the first American victory in a night battle against the IJN, one Japanese heavy cruiser and a destroyer are sunk. According to Japanese sources, the heavy cruiser is struck by one of the seven American torpedoes launched, the first such success for the Mark 15 torpedo during the war. One American destroyer is sunk by Japanese gunfire.

November 13

First Naval Battle of Guadalcanal. American and Japanese naval units clash at short range in a vicious night battle. American torpedoes prove ineffective: 14 torpedoes are fired at close range at the lead Japanese battleship but none hits or explodes, and although 26 other torpedoes are launched, only two of these hit a possible target. Japanese launch 72 Type 93 torpedoes with at least six hitting their target, sinking two destroyers, sinking or damaging two light cruisers, and damaging a heavy cruiser.

November 15

Second Naval Battle of Guadalcanal. Type 93 torpedoes hit three American destroyers, sinking two, but none fired at the two American battleships present hits their target. Thus undamaged, one of the American battleships sinks the only Japanese battleship present, gaining a major victory for the US Navy.

November 30

The battle of Tassafaronga. In the most stunning display yet of the power of the Type 93 torpedo, 28 are launched at an American cruiser force. Three heavy cruisers are damaged and one sunk. Twenty Mark 15 torpedoes are launched by American destroyers with no result. Of the eight Japanese destroyers engaged, only one is sunk.

1943

March 26 The battle of the Komandorski Islands in the North Pacific. A force of one American heavy cruiser, one light cruiser, and four destroyers engage a Japanese force of two heavy, two light cruisers, and three destroyers: 42 or 43 Type 93 and five Mark 15 torpedoes are launched with no hits scored by either side. Gunfire damages three American and two Japanese ships, but none are sunk.

July 6 The battle of Kula Gulf. An American force of three light cruisers and four destroyers intercepts a Japanese transport force of ten destroyers. Two Japanese destroyers are sunk and five damaged, but the Japanese torpedo and sink a light cruiser.

July 13 The battle of Kolombangara. An Allied force of three light cruisers and ten destroyers engage a Japanese force of one light cruiser and five destroyers. After losing their light cruiser to American gunfire, the Japanese destroyers torpedo all three light cruisers and sink a destroyer.

August 6–7 In the battle of Vella Gulf, six American destroyers engage four Japanese destroyers. Three Japanese ships are sunk by torpedoes in this first-ever American destroyer victory.

August 18 In the battle off Horaniu, each side commits four destroyers. Neither side suffers any ships sunk in this inconclusive action.

October 6 At the battle of Vella Lavella, three American destroyers intercept a Japanese force of six destroyers. One of the American destroyers is sunk by torpedoes and the other two are damaged. The Japanese lose one destroyer.

November 2 The battle of Empress Augusta Bay. A Japanese force of two heavy cruisers, two light cruisers, and six destroyers attempt to attack the American beachhead on Bougainville Island. They are engaged by four American light cruisers and eight destroyers. The Japanese are repulsed for the loss of a light cruiser and a destroyer; no American ships are sunk.

November 25 At the battle of Cape St. George, the final battle of the Solomons campaign, five American destroyers engage five Japanese destroyers. Three Japanese destroyers are lost and no American ship is even damaged.

Fubuki pictured in 1931. The power of this ship can be seen in its three Type A twin 5in gun mounts and the three triple torpedo mounts. *Fubuki* remained a front-line unit into the Pacific War and was sunk by gunfire at the battle of Cape Esperance in October 1942. (Yamato Museum)

This beam view of Fletcher-class unit *Charles Ausburne* while operating in the Solomons shows the powerful and balanced appearance of these ships. The class had five 5in guns and two quintuple torpedo launchers. (NHHC NH 59856)

DESIGN AND DEVELOPMENT

DESTROYER DESIGN PRINCIPLES AND DOCTRINE

THE US NAVY

The period between the wars was marked by multiple international naval treaties. While these were more restrictive in regards to the construction and modification of capital ships, they also affected the construction of destroyers. This was especially evident after the London Naval Treaty of 1930, which for the first time put limits on overall destroyer construction and restricted the maximum size of destroyers. Now naval planners were faced with difficult choices. Basically, they could opt for a small number of larger destroyers with greater capabilities including heavier armament, greater endurance, and superior sea-keeping characteristics, or select a larger number of smaller ships that had to compromise on one or several of the areas mentioned above. This friction between optimal ship design and overall numbers was never resolved until treaty restrictions were cast aside, which in the case of the US Navy, did not occur until the Fletcher class of 1940.

Between the wars, American naval strategy envisioned a decisive naval engagement somewhere in the Western Pacific as the culmination of a steady naval advance toward

Fletcher-class destroyer *O'Bannon* with her forward 5in battery trained to port. A powerful main gun battery was always an important design consideration for American destroyers to enable them to perform a multitude of missions. (NHHC 80-G-K-3980)

Japan. In this construct, the decisive arm was the battle line composed of the fleet's battleships. However, destroyers had a key role to play. They had a list of missions to perform, both offensive and defensive. Offensively, they were tasked to probe enemy formations to gauge their strength and then engage in torpedo attacks once the battle was joined. The primary targets of these attacks were ideally enemy battleships since they were the central measure of naval power. This required a high tactical speed and a heavy torpedo armament. A heavy gun armament was also required to defend the destroyer from enemy light units as the destroyer closed for a torpedo attack.

There was a constant friction in American destroyer design over which to stress – gun or torpedo armament. Because of the relative lack of light cruisers, the US Navy expected that its destroyers would play a major role in defeating Japanese destroyer attacks against the battle line. This and the need to carry a dual-purpose armament to defend against Japanese air attack from island bases as the US Navy advanced across the Pacific mitigated for a strong gun armament. Nevertheless, torpedo armament could not be ignored for this was the only way a destroyer was going to inflict significant damage on heavy enemy units. Though the Americans did not see many opportunities for a destroyer to use its torpedoes in a fleet engagement, destroyers had to carry a heavy torpedo armament because of the inability to replenish torpedoes at sea. This meant that three or four quadruple launchers were carried to ensure that sufficient torpedoes were carried for two fleet engagements.

Defensively, American destroyers were tasked to screen the battle line against the expected attacks by Japanese destroyers. Destroyers would also screen the battle line and other heavy units from enemy submarines, thus an effective antisubmarine armament was required. Also during the period between the wars, the potential effect of enemy air power began to be appreciated, thus requiring that American destroyers possess some measure of defensive antiaircraft capability.

Given the requirement to operate in the Pacific where high endurance was a must – and the requirement for high speed and a heavy armament of guns, torpedoes, and some antisubmarine and antiaircraft weaponry – American designers favored large destroyer designs.

THE IJN

Like the US Navy, the IJN had put considerable thought into the nature of the expected clash between fleets. The Japanese had the problem of addressing how they would overcome the larger American Navy. Their answer was an attrition strategy that would reduce the American advantage in capital ships before the clash of battle lines. A principal part of this strategy was a night battle and operations by torpedo-equipped units to create the conditions necessary for a successful gun engagement by the Japanese battle line. Given this, destroyers and torpedo tactics figured prominently in Japanese naval thinking and strategy.

The basic element of the night battle was destroyer divisions (three–four ships each), which were formed into destroyer squadron (ideally four divisions). Each squadron was led by a light cruiser that had command spaces big enough to act as a flagship.

To carry out its night-combat strategy, the Japanese developed destroyers with high speed and heavy armament. This led to the Fubuki class or "Special Type." Most importantly, this class carried an impressive torpedo armament of nine torpedo tubes and additional reload torpedoes. This basic design precept was carried forward on the next five classes of Japanese destroyers. This also marked the Japanese destroyer as primarily an offensive weapon, maximized for its role as a night-combat torpedo platform.

NIGHT-FIGHTING DOCTRINE

THE US NAVY

The US Navy entered the war with inadequate night-fighting doctrine and capabilities. This was marked by an emphasis on gun combat and a flawed torpedo doctrine. Since gunnery was seen as the fleet's main weapon, the destroyers were kept near the heavy ships to defend them and to keep out of the way of their gunnery. To be sure, destroyers did get shots with their torpedoes in the close-range night battles around Guadalcanal, but these were usually not at optimal target angles and when a good shot offered itself, the torpedo malfunction issue came into play.

Development of night-fighting tactics began in about 1932, and these evolved much in the way Japanese night-fighting tactics did. The Americans saw the need to prepare for a decisive fleet engagement and recognized that part of it would be fought at night. At the start of the war, American night-fighting doctrine focused on what was called "Major Tactics." These were the tactics needed to gain success in the expected decisive engagement between opposing battle lines. This was at the expense of "Minor Tactics" in which light units were engaged.

The focus on the decisive battle required that cruisers and destroyers conduct a night attack on Japanese formations. The tactic for this was called "Night Search and

An American Fletcher-class destroyer engages a target with 5in gunfire. Even with flashless powder, a ship using gunfire at night became a visible target. (NHHC 80-G-54646)

Attack" in which cruisers and destroyers located and then attacked enemy battleships with torpedoes. Three phases were identified for the Night Search and Attack. In the first, destroyers would form a line abreast scouting formation to locate the enemy. Once found, cruiser and destroyer gunfire would force a gap in the enemy screen allowing the destroyers to penetrate the enemy formation. In the next phase, the destroyers located the battleships and transmitted contact reports to other friendly units. In the final phase, large numbers of destroyers would attack the enemy battleships at close range with torpedoes. Gunfire was to be used against the battleship's bridge and superstructure to diminish the effectiveness of the enemy's defensive fire. This was what was continually practiced and it reinforced the concept that only battleships were worthy of torpedo attack and that the targets would be fairly slow and well illuminated thus making good targets. Unfortunately for the Americans, this had little resemblance to the type of night combat they would face in the Solomons.

Going into the battle for Guadalcanal, the conviction that gunnery was the key to victory remained firm. From battleships on down, gunnery was viewed as the dominant factor. At night, battleships were rarely committed, so this left cruisers to provide the firepower needed for victory. Early in the Guadalcanal campaign, the firepower of the heavy cruiser was preferred as its heavier 8in shell possesed the penetrative power to defeat its Japanese counterparts. The heavy cruisers took heavy losses at Guadalcanal, and in the later phases of the campaign when Japanese destroyers were the primary adversaries, the fast-firing 6in guns on the light cruisers were preferred in night combat.

The light cruisers could blanket a target with an enormous barrage of 6in shells. Combined with radar, American admirals were convinced that they could engage a target at 10,000yd and destroy it before it could fire torpedoes. This was totally ignorant of the true capabilities of the Japanese Type 93, which had an effective range comparable to cruiser gunnery.

As American doctrine changed due to the lessons of war, the role of the destroyer remained secondary. Prewar destroyer doctrine did not apply in the Solomons, and there was nothing else to replace it. Development and refinement of doctrine was highly decentralized and often left to the individual task force commander. This was acceptable when the component units of the task force were stable and the same ships and commanders worked together for an extended period, giving them the time to become familiar with each other and to develop effective plans. However, during the Solomons campaign, ships assigned to task forces were not familiar with each other and even commanders changed frequently. Not until later in the campaign when more ships became available was it possible to introduce a higher degree of cohesion. This allowed for better preparation, the development and incorporation of better plans, and ultimately much more effective task forces.

American night-combat doctrine was also totally ignorant of the potential of American torpedoes, which had proven largely ineffective during the battle for Guadalcanal. This was a result of both bad tactics and faulty technology. Destroyer tactics were totally subservient to the cruiser; destroyers were only used to finish off cripples from cruiser gunfire or to screen the cruisers from destroyer attack. Destroyers were tied to the cruisers and not allowed to operate independently. If these bad tactics were not recognized by the American admirals fighting in the

Fubuki, a Group I Special Type destroyer, with her entire nine-tube torpedo battery trained to port. Japanese destroyers equipped with the Type 93 torpedo possessed tremendous firepower, even against heavy ships, and claimed a central role in IJN prewar tactics. (*Ships of the World* magazine)

Solomons, they were noticed by both Commander of the Pacific Fleet Chester Nimitz and Chief of Naval Operations Ernest King. Both recognized the unhealthy focus on gunnery and the ignorance of the potential of American torpedoes and the dangers presented by Japanese torpedoes. Nimitz went as far as to comment on February 15, 1943: "In no night action has our destroyers' major offensive strength, the torpedo, been used effectively."

In response to the prodding from Nimitz and King, and in response to the unquestioned success of Japanese destroyers, the Americans began to question their torpedo doctrine going into 1943. On February 20, Rear Admiral Mahlon Tisdale, the commander of the Pacific Fleet's destroyers, issued a new tactical bulletin. All Japanese ships, destroyer and above, were now seen to be suitable torpedo targets. He also ordered that the speed setting of the Mark 15 be lowered from 45 to 32kts to extend the range of the weapons to 10,000yd. This allowed the destroyers to exploit their radars and attack targets beyond visual range at night. Tisdale also ordered that the torpedoes be set at a more shallow depth.

By July 1943 all the technical faults of the Mark 15 torpedo were recognized and corrected. Once the torpedo was rendered effective, the new tactics coming into play could exploit the weapon. The combination of radar, an effective torpedo, and new tactics would make the American destroyer a potent weapon.

THE IJN

With the introduction of the long-range Type 93 torpedo, the Japanese re-worked their night-fighting tactics to take advantage of the revolutionary capabilities of the new weapon. Following a "long-distance concealed firing" by heavy cruisers, the destroyer squadrons would complete the destruction of the enemy. These maneuvers required constant practice. This included elemental training by the

IJN ARMAMENT

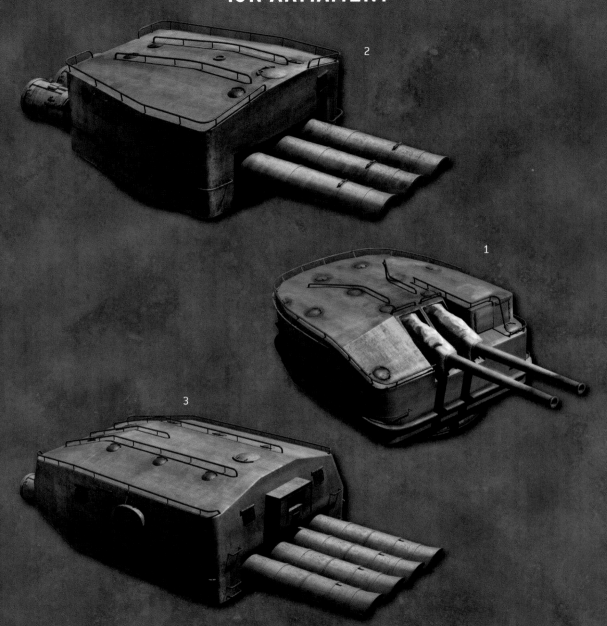

The standard gun aboard Japanese destroyers was the 5in/50 (**1**). Almost all of these were fitted in a twin-mount gunhouse, which came in four types. The Type C/D mount, shown here, was fitted on every class of fleet destroyer after the Shiratsuyu class. The mount was not armored, but did provide weather protection for the gun crew. The main weapon of a Japanese destroyer was its torpedo battery.

Shown here are a triple launcher (**2**), fitted on the Special Type and the Hatsuhara class, and the quadruple launcher (**3**) fitted to every subsequent class. Both are fitted with a shield for the crew of the torpedo mount. Doubling the effectiveness of these torpedo mounts was the fact that almost every destroyer carried reloads for every mount.

various ships themselves on the actual loading, aiming, and firing of the Type 93, but also required maneuvering formations of ships together to properly employ massed torpedo tactics.

The Japanese also put great emphasis on developing the tools required to conduct night fighting. One area of importance was in optics. In the two decades preceding the Pacific War, the Japan Optical Company produced world-class optical devices. Among these were powerful binoculars with sophisticated magnification and light-gathering capabilities. These varied in size up to 8.25in, but the Type 88 Model 1 introduced in 1932 was especially effective at night. The higher the quality and the bigger the lens, the more capable it was in low-light conditions. The superiority of Japanese optics compared to American optics went far to counterbalance the Japanese lack of radar. During the early parts of the campaign, Japanese optics actually proved superior to American electronics. The Japanese also developed star shells and flares, including a parachute-suspended type in 1935, and Japanese guns used smokeless powder to avoid disclosing the location of the firing ship.

The 1934 Battle Instructions underscored the importance of destroyer squadrons in night combat. Each destroyer squadron was supported by a division of heavy cruisers, which made up a night-combat group. The heavy cruisers provided the combat power to permit the destroyers to penetrate to attack the enemy's battle line.

By 1936, night combat was seen as an essential part of the decisive battle. The cruisers and destroyers of the Second Fleet constituted the core of the Night Battle Force. In carefully choreographed sequence, the Night Combat Force would close with and encircle the enemy. Then the heavy cruisers would open the battle with a massed torpedo assault. The culmination of the engagement was a massed attack by the destroyer squadrons at close range. The destroyers would fire their first load, then disengage, reload, and fire a second barrage.

Of course, there was no set-piece major fleet engagement in the Solomons, but the Japanese emphasis on small unit tactics translated directly to the night engagements. Destroyers were trained to approach the target at high speed, with the flagship as the guide unit. Destroyer torpedo attacks were delivered from one flank of the enemy. Targets would be deconflicted so that there was no over-concentration on a single target. Each destroyer would fire a complete torpedo salvo. The surprise torpedo attack was followed with a close-quarters attack using gunfire. Following the example of the flagship, each ship would use searchlights to illuminate the enemy. Using searchlights, destroyers would open fire at 6,500yd and close to a battle range of 3,250yd. Guns were fired only in salvos to allow lookouts to close their eyes and protect their night vision.

Doctrine was useful as a general guide for night combat, but Japanese commanders modified it during the campaign. The Japanese were fully aware of the American use of radar. Not wanting to be surprised, especially after the battle of Vella Gulf where American destroyers surprised and torpedoed three Japanese destroyers before their presence was even noted, later in the campaign Japanese commanders would fire their torpedoes as soon as they gained contact on the enemy and could get a fire solution. Following that, the Japanese would move out of range to reload torpedoes and then seek to re-engage if tactical conditions permitted. Gunfire was not favored by the Japanese, but they would immediately use it if surprised.

DESTROYER TORPEDOES

THE US NAVY

The torpedo is the classic weapon of a destroyer. The standard American destroyer torpedo of World War II was the Mark 15. The characteristics of the Mark 15 are provided below, but even if it worked as advertised, it was markedly inferior to the standard Japanese torpedo. The real problem with the Mark 15 was its reliability. The difficulties of the Mark 15 were related to those experienced by the Mark 14, which was the standard submarine-launched torpedo. Both relied on the Mark 6 magnetic exploder, which was faulty. American torpedoes also tended to run well below their set depth. The result was that American destroyers went into the Solomons campaign with a faulty weapon.

Faulty torpedoes during the initial Guadalcanal battles reinforced American naval officers' predisposition to believe that the gun, not the torpedo, was the US Navy's primary weapon of decision. Naval officers were concerned with the lack of success by destroyer-launched torpedoes, but this was explained by a number of factors – the weapons were launched at a range too close to arm, at excessive ranges, and some appeared not to explode when they hit their target.

The Mark 15 was designed for use aboard destroyers. After a number of technical faults were corrected, it became an effective weapon by mid-July 1943. (NHHC NH 84497)

This is a Mark 15 torpedo mount on a Fletcher-class destroyer in 1943. The Mark 15 mount had a circular shield while the nearly identical Mark 14 had no shield. (NHHC 80-G-K-3977)

Non-combat situations should have been a real indicator that there was a glaring technical issue with the Mark 15. At the battle of Santa Cruz, 18 torpedoes were fired at a derelict American carrier and a destroyer to scuttle them. Despite perfect conditions, only nine of these actually hit their target and exploded. The Bureau of Ordnance countered by declaring that there was no evidence of a material defect with the torpedoes.

In fact, the Mark 15 had many problems. By mid-1943, these had finally been largely corrected. The magnetic exploders were turned off by permission of Nimitz in June. The original firing pin springs were replaced by stronger ones. Torpedoes were set to run at shallower depths. This became official policy in October when all Pacific Fleet destroyers were ordered to set torpedo depth at 6ft unless the target was identified as a battleship. These remedies at least gave American destroyers weapons that worked.

THE IJN

The Japanese placed great importance on torpedo tactics practiced by their destroyers, which were required to close with the enemy to maximize the chances of success. This was a hazardous undertaking at night, and even more so during the day. If a torpedo could be developed that could be fired at long range, this would revolutionize torpedo tactics.

In order to improve the speed and range of their torpedoes, the Japanese determined they would have to use a new source of energy. By replacing all the nitrogen in the torpedo propellant with oxygen, they expected a heat energy increase of as much as four times. The use of compressed oxygen also increased the space available for the warhead and another desirable side effect was that an oxygen torpedo offered nearly wakeless running.

However, deciding to use highly compressed oxygen as an energy source was different to actually mastering the technology to make it possible. Using oxygen as

The Japanese Type 93 surface-launched torpedo was a fearsome weapon nearly 30ft long and weighing almost 3 tons. This particular weapon was recovered off Guadalcanal and is shown displayed in Washington, DC, later in the war. The failure of the US Navy to recognize that the Japanese had developed a torpedo with far greater performance than the best American torpedo was the basis for severe American losses in the Solomons campaign. (NHHC NH 94125)

a propellant is dangerous since pure oxygen reacts violently to many materials, including oil and grease. This makes using it dangerous in a shipboard environment. The major technical issue was explosions at the instant of ignition, which were caused by extremely high temperatures when the pure oxygen was introduced. This was solved by the use of a small starting air chamber located near the oxygen tank that used natural air and sea water (instead of fresh water). The oxygen was gradually introduced to replace the air. This system was successfully tested in the summer of 1932 and the design for the actual production model was completed by the end of 1932. Despite the fact that the torpedo did not enter service until 1935, it was adopted as the Type 93 in 1933 (the designation comes from the fact that the year 1933 is the year 2593 on the Japanese calendar).

The Type 93 was eventually fitted on all modern destroyers, heavy cruisers, and select light cruisers. It was considered a top-secret weapon within the IJN, and not surprisingly, its existence was unknown to the Americans at the start of the war. The table below shows the clear superiority of the Type 93 over its American counterpart.

American and Japanese destroyer-launched torpedoes		
	Mark 15 (USN)	Type 93 (IJN)
Length:	22ft 7in	29ft 6in
Diameter:	21in	24in
Weight:	3,438lb	5,940lb
Warhead:	494lb	1,078lb
Propulsion:	Steam	Oxygen
Speed:	28/34/46kts	36/40/48kts
Range:	15,000/10,000/6,000yd	43,700/35,000/21,900yd

This is a view of *Mahan* in 1944 showing the two forward 5in guns with partial shields and the Mark 33 fire-control director above the bridge. (NHHC 19-N-67752)

USN ARMAMENT

The primary American destroyer gun was the redoubtable 5in/38 dual-purpose gun (**1**). Almost all American destroyers carried these in single-mounts. Many were not equipped with shields or only fitted with half-shields in an effort to reduce top weight. This is the Mark 30/18 shielded power-worked single base mounting fitted to several classes of destroyers including, most notably, the Fletcher class. The 5in/38 was the most effective dual-purpose gun of the war.

American destroyers were fitted with either quadruple (**2**) or quintuple tube mounts (**3**). The quintuple tube mounts were fitted to every class starting with the Benson class. The Fletcher class had two quintuple mounts fitted, which were retained throughout the war even as improved antiaircraft armament became a priority. Unlike Japanese destroyers, American ships were not provided with torpedo reloads.

1

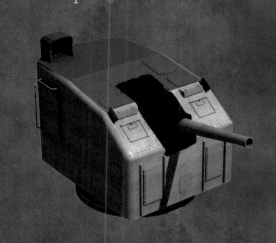

2

3

As impressive as the Type 93 was, it was not perfect. It had a tendency to explode early, often when the torpedo's sensitive fuse hit a ship's wake or other turbulence. This warned enemy ships they were under attack. Accuracy at long ranges was not good.

The Japanese also stressed the development of a fire-control system that could allow them to employ the Type 93 at long range. For destroyers, the Type 97 director was employed and was linked to a 4.7in binocular-type sight. The Type 3 Model 2 target courses and speed instrument allowed the ship to fire its torpedoes blind after the target was lost from view.

Incredibly, despite a string of battles in which the Type 93 figured prominently, the US Navy did not issue a formal intelligence bulletin describing its performance accurately until March 1944.

DESTROYER GUNS

THE US NAVY

Every American destroyer built between the wars and during the war employed the 5in gun in its main battery. The 5in/38 was an excellent weapon with a good range and a high rate of fire. It was a true dual-purpose weapon, but was actually maximized for high angle use against aircraft. It was equipped with an elaborate fire-control system for the day, which contributed to top weight problems on several classes.

It was probably the best dual-purpose gun of the war. While shell weight and muzzle velocity were average, it was above average in rate of fire, reliability, accuracy, and rate of training and elevation. Many different types of mounts were provided for destroyers. Most were single gun mounts, and most were enclosed, though open and

partially shielded mounts with weather resistant canvas tops were also fitted. The shield was only 3.18mm thick, barely enough for some degree of shrapnel protection.

5in/38 gun on Mark 30 mount	
Shell weight:	55lb
Muzzle velocity:	2,600ft/sec
Firing cycle:	2.7 seconds
Maximum range:	18,200yd at 45-degree elevation

THE IJN

The standard Japanese 5in destroyer gun dated from 1914. It was deployed in single and twin mounts in several different types. The first ten of the Fubuki class were fitted with the Type A twin mount with a maximum 40-degree elevation. The later ships of the class introduced the Type B mount, which had a 75-degree elevation in an attempt

Fletcher-class destroyer *Nicholas*, shown here in January 1944, saw considerable action during the Solomons campaign participating in the battles of Kula Gulf, Kolombangara, and Horaniu. This view shows her radar fit including the SC on top of the foremast, the curved SG just below it, and the Mark 4 on top of the Mark 37 fire-control director. (NHHC 19-N-61786)

to make the mounts capable of antiaircraft fire. However, training and elevation were so slow that these mounts were useless for this role. The Shiratsuyu class introduced the Type C mount with 55-degree elevation; this was also the standard mount on the next two classes. The new Type D mount with a 75-degree elevation was introduced on the Yugumo class.

This weapon was a solid design with a range actually greater than its American counterpart, but with a much slower rate of fire. The Japanese 5in guns were never really capable of dual-purpose employment, which became increasingly important as Japanese destroyers were exposed to American air attack. The twin mount also had a dispersion problem when employed against surface targets. The shields were only 3mm thick.

5in/50 3rd Year (1914) gun	
Shell weight:	50.7lb
Muzzle velocity:	2,986–3,002ft/sec
Firing cycle:	6–12 seconds
Maximum range:	20,100yd

USN RADAR SCREEN

This view shows the radar return of a USN Mark 4 radar. This radar was mounted on top of the Mark 33 or Mark 37 fire-control directors aboard American destroyers which provided fire control for the ship's 5in battery. The Mark 4 proved effective in service, especially in the hands of an experienced operator. The operator selected a range gate, usually 500–1,000yd in width, which ensured only signals from the intended target were displayed. The two separate antenna of the Mark 4 transmitted two beams at slightly different angles. The returns from these two beams were displayed side-by-side on the operator's scope, as shown here. To keep the director pointed at the target, the operator had to keep the two beams at an equal height, as shown in this example. Despite difficulties in breaking out targets close to land and correctly ranging on two ships placed close together, the Mark 4 provided American gun crews with the capability to engage targets at night and in poor visibility conditions. This greatly increased the effectiveness of destroyer gunfire and the Japanese had nothing similar.

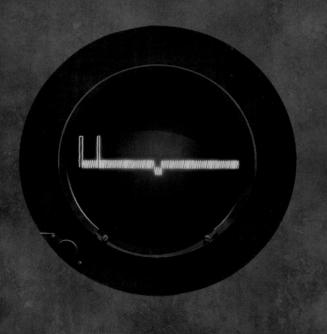

RADAR

The impact of radar on the night surface battles fought in the Solomons cannot be overstated. At the start of the campaign, most American ships were radar-equipped and the Japanese were not. However, early American radars were unreliable and their operators and commanders did not understand how to work them or how to best exploit them in combat.

The first radar fitted aboard destroyers was the SC-2 radar. This was a large rectangular "bed spring" antenna positioned at the top of the main mast. This was used primarily as an air search radar. Installation began in late 1941 and in January 1942 a new version was introduced with twice the power. Range was approximately 20nm on a battleship and 6nm on a destroyer-sized target. Accuracy was 100yd and 5 degrees.

Newer destroyers arrived in the Pacific fitted with the SG radar. Usually, this was fitted below the SC radar on the mainmast. The SG had a smaller convex antenna and was designed as a surface search radar. It was the first American S-band radar and had a narrow 3-degree beamwidth with minimal sidelobes. It was also the first surface search set to incorporate a plan position indicator (PPI) display. The PPI provided a radar "map" of the area and was much easier to use and interpret. It gave both a range and bearing to the target, which showed as bright spots on the screen. The SG/SG-1 became standard for destroyers. Approximate detection range was

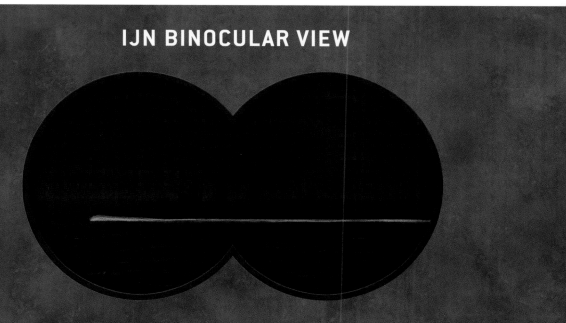

IJN BINOCULAR VIEW

This view is what a Japanese look-out might see through his Type 88 Model 1 binoculars as his ship entered waters thought to contain enemy ships. In this case, the alert crewman has detected an American Fletcher-class destroyer. So effective were Japanese night optics that they often outperformed American electronics, especially the earlier SC radars. The ability of the Japanese to visually sight American ships at extended ranges was vitally important since the side which converted early detection into an opening torpedo salvo was usually victorious in the destroyer battles of 1943.

This May 1946 shot of *Yukikaze* shows the bridge structure of the Kagero class. The device on top of the bridge is the fire-control director for the 5in battery. The twin-horn Type 22 radar is mounted above on the foremast. Of the 19 units of the Kagero class, only *Yukikaze* survived the war. She ended her days in Nationalist Chinese service. (*Ships of the World* magazine)

22nm for a battleship-sized target and 15nm against a destroyer. Accuracy was 200yd and 2 degrees.

Though the SG did change the way the Americans fought night battles, there were still problems. One was that it was unable to discern different targets located close together or maneuvering rapidly. The bigger problem was that the SG radar could not discern between ships and shell splashes around ships after American guns had taken the target under fire.

In addition to the SG and SC radars, destroyers carried the Mark 4 fire-control radar mounted on top of the Mark 33 or Mark 37 fire-control director for the 5in battery. This was the first American dual-purpose radar able to engage surface and air targets. Overall, it proved very successful except when conducting blind fire. The operator selected a range gate, usually 500–1,000yd in width, which ensured only signals from the target were displayed. The radar transmitted two separate beams each just off the direct line of sight to the target. The returns from these two beams were displayed side-by-side on the operator's scope. The operator would then move the director to keep the two beams on equal height on his scope. This indicated that the director was pointed directly at the target.

The use of radar revolutionized fire control. No longer did night or poor visibility blind the gunner. However, the process described above worked well when a single target was being engaged by a single ship. When there were two targets in the range gate and both were discernible, the operator tended to split the difference between them and point the director accordingly. The most prevalent problem was when shell splashes were created around the target since the radar could not tell the difference between the splashes and the target. This quickly decreased the accuracy of radar-controlled gunnery since shell splashes in front of the target were often the strongest returns, which prompted the operator to target the splashes. This led to the phenomenon known as "chasing splashes," which drew the gunnery increasingly off target as the real target moved away. When the ship finally stopped targeting its own splashes, the return disappeared, leading to the assessment that the target had been sunk. When the original target was subsequently picked up again, it appeared as a new target, making it hard for the commander to get a real count of the number of enemy ships present. During the Solomons campaign, the Americans learned that the maximum effective range for radar-controlled gunnery was 10,000yd.

The Japanese had no radar, at least not until mid-1943 when select Japanese destroyers finally received the No. 22 radar. This was designed for surface search. It was a twin-horn set, one for transmitting and one for receiving. It was mounted on the foremast of destroyers. Against a destroyer-sized target, the No. 22 was supposedly effective out to 18,591yd. The range error was 820–1,640ft and the bearing error up to 3 degrees. The radar was not accurate enough to provide for control of gunnery. Early Japanese radars were unreliable and their operators often poorly trained. In order to compensate for the lack of radar, the Japanese had to rely on their superior optics, training, and tactics. In an attempt to negate the American advantage in radar, the Japanese equipped their destroyers with radar detection gear, but the results do not appear to have been favorable. The American technological advantage became increasingly problematic for the Japanese when the Americans gained confidence in their use of radar and adopted new tactics. It would not be an overestimation to state that radar was the single most important factor leading to the demise of the Japanese destroyer force.

THE STRATEGIC
SITUATION

With the end of the battle for Guadalcanal in February 1943, the Americans planned to advance into the Central Solomons with the intention of eventually neutralizing or occupying the key Japanese base at Rabaul on New Britain Island. Following landings on New Georgia in the Central Solomons to gain additional air bases, the next objective was to land on Bougainville Island in the Northern Solomons. Once established this close to Rabaul, the Americans could make Japanese use of their Rabaul bases untenable.

By 1943, the Americans had opened a war on two fronts. The drive up the Solomons continued and Nimitz opened a new drive through the Central Pacific. This double approach strategy kept the Japanese off-guard. To conduct the advance up the Solomons, Vice Admiral William F. Halsey commanded the Third Fleet, which was newly created on March 15, 1943 from the former South Pacific Command. This was a balanced force with two carrier forces, a fast battleship group, a force of some of the old battleships and new escort carriers. These were only committed for major operations or held in reserve for an appearance by the Combined Fleet. The majority of the operations were assigned to the amphibious force and two mixed light cruiser–destroyer forces. Each was assigned four light cruisers and eight destroyers. These were the forces assigned to protect the amphibious forces and intercept Japanese forces as they attempted to attack American beachheads or move reinforcements to various points in the Solomons. After a series of night engagements between these cruiser–destroyer forces and Japanese destroyer forces in which the Americans fared badly, it became preferred to only commit destroyers against Japanese destroyers. With the

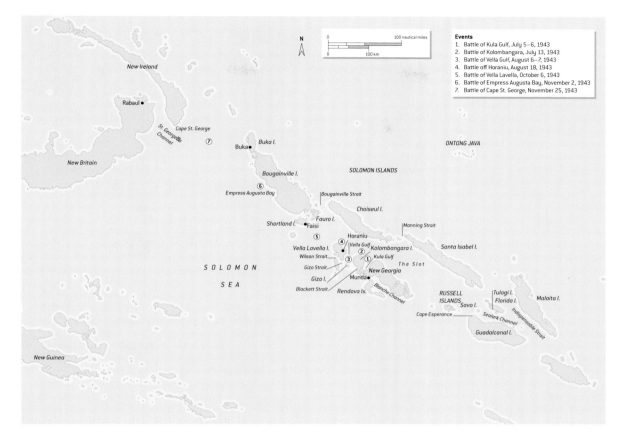

The following is the content inside the map image:

Events
1. Battle of Kula Gulf, July 5–6, 1943
2. Battle of Kolombangara, July 13, 1943
3. Battle of Vella Gulf, August 6–7, 1943
4. Battle off Horaniu, August 18, 1943
5. Battle of Vella Lavella, October 6, 1943
6. Battle of Empress Augusta Bay, November 2, 1943
7. Battle of Cape St. George, November 25, 1943

The Central and Northern Solomon Islands.

flood of American naval production now reaching the Pacific, Halsey had the ability to form several destroyer groups to take up the fight against Japanese light forces.

American destroyer squadrons were typically assigned two destroyer divisions. At full strength, a squadron could contain up to nine destroyers. At the start of the Solomons campaign, the only destroyers available were the prewar classes. By November 1942, the fruits of war production were evident with the arrival of the first Fletcher-class destroyers. Increasingly, these were committed to front-line duties and the surviving older destroyers relegated to escort duties. By the end of 1943, the Fletcher class was carrying the bulk of the front-line duties.

Since the mid-November 1942 battles off Guadalcanal, the IJN had largely decided that it was unwise to risk major ships (heavy cruiser and battleships) in further night battles in waters dominated by American airpower during the day. Any units damaged at night (and in a confusing night engagement anything could happen) were likely to be lost since Japanese airpower was dwindling and could not provide adequate cover. This left it to the IJN's destroyer forces to conduct the majority of operations in the Solomons.

The reluctance to commit heavy ships was bad enough, but commander of the Combined Fleet Yamamoto Isoroku was also parsimonious in his allocation of destroyers to the Eighth Fleet. This lack of decisiveness meant the Japanese were fighting a poor man's war in the Solomons even though on paper, the Combined Fleet

29

maintained superior forces at the Central Pacific anchorage at Truk, some 800 miles north of Rabaul. Yamamoto, and later his replacement after his death in April 1943, both failed to realize that the decisive battle they were hoping and planning for was taking place in the Solomons.

The Eighth Fleet, based at Rabaul, was assigned responsibility to contest the American advance in the Solomons. Its commander from April 1, 1943 was Vice Admiral Samejima Tomoshige who replaced Vice Admiral Mikawa Gunichi. Japanese strategy called for an immediate counterattack wherever the Americans landed. What this meant was that the destroyers were compelled to continue to conduct transport, reinforcement, and supply duties for the Japanese garrisons in the Solomons.

The Eighth Fleet was understrength to perform its mission. In March 1943, it was assigned fleet flagship heavy cruiser *Chokai* and Destroyer Squadron 3. This squadron was assigned light cruiser *Sendai* and Destroyer Divisions 11, 22, and 30. Only Destroyer Division 11 was assigned modern units of the Fubuki class.

Each destroyer squadron was assigned a light cruiser as its flagship and each division was supposed to have three or four ships. This was not the case by mid-1943 when attrition and the requirement for overhauls following incessant operations typically reduced a division to one or two ships. The IJN's destroyer formations were being run into the ground. Throughout the campaign, the Japanese fed reinforcements into the struggle. In July, Destroyer Squadron 2 with a division of new Kagero-class destroyers entered the fray. By August, Destroyer Divisions 4 (Asashio class), 17 (Kagero class), and 27 (Hatsuhara and Shiratsuyu classes) were also committed. In October 1943, *Sentai* 5 (a squadron of Myoko-class heavy cruisers) and Destroyer Squadron 10 were assigned to the Eighth Fleet. Nevertheless, the average number of operational destroyers at Rabaul was rarely more than ten.

TECHNICAL
SPECIFICATIONS

US NAVY DESTROYERS

The Americans entered World War II with a mix of "four-stacker" destroyers from World War I, two classes of destroyer leaders, and several classes of 1,500-ton ships. The epitome of American destroyer design, the Fletcher class, did not reach the Pacific theater until late in the Guadalcanal campaign. By the time of the destroyer clashes in 1943, this was the most numerous destroyer in the Pacific Fleet and was the American destroyer crews' preferred ship in which to go into harm's way.

This December 1943 view of *Farragut* shows the basic layout of this class with its four single 5in mounts and two quadruple torpedo mounts. After an active war career in the Pacific, *Farragut* was sold for scrap in 1947. (NHHC 80-G-321652)

THE FARRAGUT CLASS

The eight-ship Farragut class was the first American destroyer class built since 1921. The design was a great advance over the old 1,190-ton "four-stacker" design. It set the template for future prewar American destroyer designs. Main armament was five of the excellent 5in/38 dual-purpose guns with a fire-control director (the Mark 33) superior to Japanese ships. Torpedo armament was eight tubes in two quadruple launchers. All eight ships saw action in the Pacific, but only three served in the Solomons, all in 1942.

The Farragut class
Total ships in class: 8
Displacement: 1,395 tons standard; 2,335 tons full load
Dimensions: length 341ft (overall); beam 34ft; draft 9ft
Maximum speed: 36.5kts
Endurance: 5,800nm at 15kts
Crew: 250

THE PORTER CLASS

The eight-ship Porter class was the first American class of destroyers designed as "destroyer leaders." To provide the space for embarked staff and the extra armament needed to act in this capacity, the design was set at 1,850 tons, the maximum permitted under the London Naval Treaty. As built, the class was fitted with eight 5in/38 low-angle guns arranged in four twin mounts. Of the eight ships, five served in the Pacific, four of these as destroyer squadron flagships. One was sunk off Guadalcanal in 1942. The only other destroyer leaders built by the American Navy were the five-ship Somers class. These were armed much like the Porter class. All five spent all or most of their careers in the Atlantic.

The Porter class
Total ships in class: 8
Displacement: 1,834 tons standard; 2,597 tons full load
Dimensions: length 381ft (overall); beam 37ft; draft 13ft
Maximum speed: 37kts
Endurance: 6,500nm at 12kts
Crew: 194

The Porter class was the first American attempt to build a destroyer leader. This is the lead ship of the class in November 1941 showing its impressive armament of four twin 5in/38 gun mounts and a total of eight torpedo tubes. Of the eight ships in the class, all except *Porter* survived the war. *Porter* was sunk at the battle of Santa Cruz in October 1942. (NHHC 19-N-26239)

THE MAHAN CLASS

The Mahan class returned to the standard 1,500-ton size. This design was able to increase the numbers of torpedo tubes to 12 in three quadruple mounts; however, the arrangement of the mounts permitted only an eight-torpedo broadside. Five single 5in/38 dual-purpose guns were also fitted even with the increase in torpedo armament. This class also introduced a high-pressure steam plant. These were the best of the US Navy's 1,500-ton designs. All 18 ships served in the Pacific. Two were sunk in the night battles off Guadalcanal in November 1942.

The Mahan class
Total ships in class: 18
Displacement: 1,488 tons standard; 2,103 tons full load
Dimensions: length 341ft (overall); beam 35ft; draft 12ft
Maximum speed: 36.5kts
Endurance: 6,500nm at 12kts
Crew: 158

This April 1942 view of *Mahan* shows the ship after an overhaul in which the No. 3 5in mount was removed. Still in place are four single 5in/38 mounts and 12 torpedo tubes. (NHHC 19-N-29528)

THE GRIDLEY CLASS

The four-ship Gridley class reflected pressures to increase the torpedo armament of American destroyers. This was accomplished by fitting four quadruple mounts (still

Gridley-class destroyer *Maury* photographed when first completed in mid-1938. The original print has been autographed by Arleigh A. Burke, who served with *Maury* while he was a destroyer division commander in 1943. *Maury* saw action in the battle of Vella Gulf. (NHHC NH 42150)

Bagley under way, c. 1937–40. The 12 units of the Bagley class were externally similar to the preceding Gridley class with four single 5in/38 mounts and four quadruple torpedo mounts. This class was heavily involved in the Solomons campaign. (NHHC NH 97726)

only providing an eight-torpedo broadside) but with the loss of a single 5in gun. The four remaining 5in/38 guns were fitted in single mounts, two forward and two aft. One of the four ships served in the Guadalcanal campaign, and two were involved in subsequent battles in the Solomons.

The Gridley class
Total ships in class: 4
Displacement: 1,590 tons standard; 2,219 tons full load
Dimensions: length 341ft (overall); beam 36ft; draft 13ft
Maximum speed: 38.5kts
Endurance: 6,500nm at 12kts
Crew: 158

THE BAGLEY CLASS

The eight-ship Bagley class was externally similar to the Gridley class. Armament was the same. These ships were all active in the Pacific, with two being sunk and four damaged during the Guadalcanal campaign.

The Bagley class
Total ships in class: 12
Displacement: 1,646 tons standard; 2,245 tons full load
Dimensions: length 341ft (overall); beam 36ft; draft 13ft
Maximum speed: 38.5kts
Endurance: 6,500nm at 12kts
Crew: 158

THE SIMS CLASS

Construction of the 12 ships of the Sims class began in 1937, after the expiration of the London Naval Treaty of 1930. This allowed its designers to increase the size of the hull and to consider expanding the armament. When the first units were completed, they were fitted with four single 5in/38 guns and three quadruple torpedo mounts. In

Sims shown in May 1940. The ships of this class were originally designed to carry five 5in guns (as shown in this view) and three quadruple torpedo tubes. Before being built, the third bank of torpedo tubes was deleted, and by 1942, the No. 3 5in gun was also removed. (NHHC 19-N-21806)

this condition, the design was seriously overweight, forcing the removal of the third bank of torpedoes and other weight-saving measures. Nine of the ships were moved to the Pacific after the Pearl Harbor attack. One was lost at Coral Sea and another at Midway. Two more were lost during the Guadalcanal campaign.

The Sims class
Total ships in class: 12
Displacement: 1,764 tons standard; 2,313 tons full load
Dimensions: length 348ft (overall); beam 36ft; draft 13ft
Maximum speed: 35kts
Endurance: 6,500nm at 12kts
Crew: 192

THE BENHAM CLASS

This class used the hull lines of the Mahan class, and a generally similar overall arrangement. The usual four single 5in/38 mounts were retained, but torpedo armament was increased to 16 tubes in four quadruple mounts. These were situated two on each beam so that the maximum torpedo broadside was eight. Most of this

Benham-class destroyers were originally designed with four quadruple banks of torpedoes, but two were later removed as in this 1943 view of Sterett. She saw action at the battle of Vella Gulf. (NHHC 80-G-321653)

class began the war assigned to the Atlantic fleet. By mid-1942, six were in the Pacific. One was damaged in and another sunk in the November night battles off Guadalcanal. Three units were active in the 1943 destroyer battles in the Central Solomons.

The Benham class
Total ships in class: 10
Displacement: 1,637 tons standard; 2,250 tons full load
Dimensions: length 341ft (overall); beam 36ft; draft 13ft
Maximum speed: 38.5kts
Endurance: 6,500nm at 12kts
Crew: 184

THE BENSON CLASS

All 24 ships of this class were commissioned before the war. This class incorporated many of the design characteristics of the Fletcher class. The class rose in displacement due to heavier machinery and a stronger hull. The arrangements of the machinery spaces were altered, which improved survivability. Five single 5in/38 dual-purpose mounts were fitted. For the first time, a quintuple torpedo mount was adopted and fitted on the centerline. With two of these mounts, this class had an impressive broadside of ten torpedoes. In early 1942, it was decided to remove one of the 5in mounts in favor of an increased antiaircraft armament. Of the 24 ships, only four saw action in the Pacific. Of these, two were sunk off Guadalcanal in 1942 and the third in 1943 in the battle of Kolombangara.

The Benson class
Total ships in class: 24
Displacement: 1,839 tons standard; 2,395 tons full load
Dimensions: length 348ft (overall); beam 36ft; draft 13ft
Maximum speed: 35kts
Endurance: 6,500nm at 12kts
Crew: 208

THE BRISTOL CLASS

In 1940, with war looming, the US Navy was compelled to take immediate steps to increase its numbers of destroyers. The easiest way to do this was to simply continue the construction of the Benson class. Eventually, 72 of the slightly modified Bristol class were ordered. None were completed before the outbreak of war in the Pacific, and construction actually continued into 1943. The quintuple torpedo mounts were retained and almost all were completed to the four-5in gun design. The majority of this class served in the Atlantic, but 24 eventually found their way to the Pacific. Seven fought in the Guadalcanal campaign with three being sunk and three damaged.

Gwin, a Benson-class unit, shown as completed in 1941. Note the battery of five 5in guns and two quintuple torpedo tubes. *Gwin* was sunk at the battle of Kolombangara by a Japanese destroyer-launched torpedo. (NHHC NH 51094)

USS *CHARLES AUSBURNE*

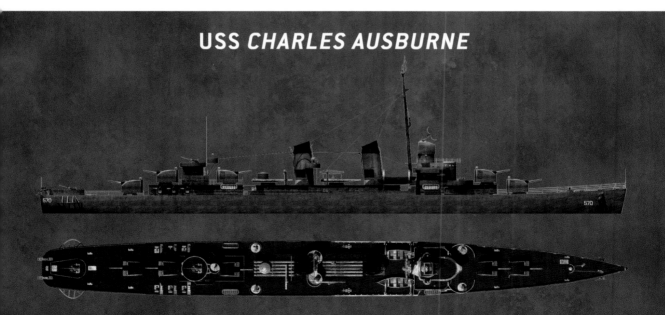

This destroyer was the flagship of Captain Burke at Cape St. George. *Charles Ausburne* was a member of the Fletcher class, the most numerous destroyer class built by the US Navy and arguably the best destroyer class of the war.

Duncan was a Bristol-class destroyer. The ship is pictured on October 7, 1942. Five days later, she was sunk at the battle of Cape Esperance. The ship's configuration features four 5in guns and five torpedo tubes. (NHHC NH 90495)

The Bristol class

Total ships in class: 72

Displacement: 1,839 tons standard; 2,395 tons full load

Dimensions: length 348ft (overall); beam 36ft; draft 13ft

Maximum speed: 35kts

Endurance: 6,500nm at 12kts

Crew: 208

THE FLETCHER CLASS

This was the first class of American destroyer built completely free of treaty restrictions and its design took advantage of wartime lessons. The first ship was not ordered until mid-1940, and the first did not reach the Pacific until late 1942. The ship was much bigger than previous designs and therefore allowed the machinery for a high maximum speed (38kts), a strong gun and torpedo armament, and even some protective plating to key areas like the bridge, command, and machinery areas. The main battery was five 5in/38 mounts able to conduct dual-purpose fire guided by the excellent Mark 37 director. Another important improvement was the ability to accept additional antiaircraft guns without sacrificing any of the 5in mounts or torpedoes. Torpedo armament was two quintuple mounts with no reloads. These ships were sent to the Pacific, and eventually 18 were lost, but only four through 1943. These were easily the best American destroyers of the first part of the war and possessed a fine balance of speed and offensive and defensive capabilities.

The Fletcher class

Total ships in class: 175

Displacement: 2,325 tons standard; 2,924 tons full load

Dimensions: length 391ft (overall); beam 40ft; draft 14ft

Maximum speed: 35kts

Endurance: 6,500nm at 15kts

Crew: 273

IJN DESTROYERS

THE FUBUKI AND AKATSUKI CLASSES

When they entered service beginning in 1928, the first units of the Fubuki class, also known as the Special Type, were the most powerful destroyers in the world. In speed, endurance, and especially in firepower, these ships were superior to their foreign rivals and set the tone for future Japanese destroyer construction up through the Yugumo class. After much debate on the proper size of the future fleet destroyer, the IJN settled on a 1,750-ton design for a 35kt, heavily armed destroyer. The principal weapon was nine 24in torpedo tubes. Notably, each of these was provided with a reload, which greatly increased the power of the ship in combat. The principal gun armament was six 5in guns in twin mounts. For the first time ever, these were placed in weatherproof gunhouses.

As usual in the naval treaty era, Japanese designers had attempted to put too much on too small a hull. Efforts to save weight on the design had been partly successful, but when the first ship of the class entered service in 1928, the ship was dangerously top-heavy and the use of light alloys and welding made the ships vulnerable to storm damage. This was demonstrated in 1935 when ten Special Type destroyers received varying degrees of storm damage. The class was modified in 1937–38, and emerged as fully effective units. Part of the price paid for reducing the top-heaviness issue was to reduce the number of torpedo reloads to six.

A total of 24 units were produced in three groups, with the four ships of Group III actually given a new class name (Akatsuki). At the start of the war, the 23 remaining ships (one was sunk by collision in 1934) were still considered front-line units. They formed five destroyer divisions and saw heavy action from the outbreak of war. The class was heavily engaged in the Solomons campaign and four were lost around Guadalcanal in 1942, and another three in the Solomons and the Bismarck Sea during 1943.

Fletcher at anchor in Purvis Bay, Florida Island, Solomon Islands, on March 26, 1943. *Fletcher* participated in the First Naval Battle of Guadalcanal and the battle of Tassafaronga during the Solomons campaign. There is no doubt that the numbers and capabilities of the Fletcher class made it the most important US destroyer class of World War II. (NHHC NH 53916)

39

Hatsuyuki was another early Special Type destroyer. The large bridge structure is evident in this 1930 view. The number on the bow is the ship's parent destroyer division and the ship's name was displayed on the side of the hull. *Hatsuyuki* was sunk by aircraft off Bougainville in July 1943. (Yamato Museum)

The Fubuki and Akatsuki classes
Total ships in class: 24
Displacement: 1,750 tons standard (Akatsuki class 1,680 tons)
Dimensions: length 389ft (overall); beam 34ft; draft 11ft
Maximum speed: 35kts (Akatsuki class 37kts)
Endurance: 5,000nm at 14kts
Crew: 197

THE HATSUHARA CLASS

After the large Special Type destroyers, the Japanese were forced to return to building smaller designs. This was dictated by the London Naval Treaty of 1930, which for the first time put limits on destroyer construction. Total Japanese destroyer tonnage was 105,500 tons and the maximum limit for a destroyer was 1,850 tons. These were considered destroyer leaders and only 16 percent of the total tonnage could be composed of ships that large. The balance of destroyer construction was to be ships of only 1,500 tons.

The approach of the IJN when faced with treaty restrictions was to jam as much as possible into as small a hull as possible. The inevitable result was overweight designs that had to be modified before being considered successful. This was the case with the Hatsuhara class, which was laid down beginning in 1931 and commissioned beginning in 1935. The employment of weight-saving measures produced a ship with five 5in

Ariake, a unit of the Hatsuhara class, pictured in 1935 after modifications to correct instability problems. The ship still retained a battery of five 5in guns (the twin mount is visible forward, and a second twin mount and a single mount were positioned aft) and two triple torpedo mounts. *Ariake* was destroyed by aircraft after running aground off Cape Gloucester on Bougainville in July 1943. (Yamato Museum)

guns and a broadside of nine torpedoes mounted in three triple launchers. All this was achieved on a design displacement 260 tons less than the Special Type ships.

In service, the class proved to be overweight and top-heavy, which prompted a major reconstruction from 1935 through 1937. What finally emerged was still a very powerful ship with six torpedo tubes and six reloads. Of note, these were the first ships fitted with the Type 93 torpedo. The main gun battery was comprised of five 5in guns with the armament arranged in a dual mount forward and a dual and a single mount aft. Speed was reduced to 33.5kts after the addition of extra weight to improve stability.

The six-ship class made up two destroyer divisions at the start of the war, and in the July 1942 reorganization of the Combined Fleet, two ships were assigned to Destroyer Division 27, which fought in the Solomons. Both of these ships were sunk in July 1943 by aircraft.

The Hatsuhara class
Total ships in class: 6
Displacement: 1,490 tons standard; 1,802 tons full load
Dimensions: length 359ft (overall); beam 33ft; draft 10ft
Maximum speed: 33.5kts
Endurance: 6,000nm at 15kts
Crew: 228

THE SHIRATSUYU CLASS

The stability problems that forced the redesign of the Hatsuhara class also forced the final six units of the class to be canceled. After the Japanese fixed the problems, the six ships re-emerged as a new class, named the Shiratsuyu class. Construction of the class began in late 1933, and ten had been commissioned by mid-1937.

The class was essentially a repeat of the Hatsuhara class, but with some differences. The torpedo armament was enhanced by the adoption of a quadruple launcher; two were fitted and both provided with a set of reloads. The number and arrangement of the gun armament was unaltered. The bridge structure was reduced to save weight and the speed increased slightly to 34kts.

Yamakaze, a member of the Shiratsuyu class, shows the layout of her main armament in this 1937 view. A twin 5in mount is positioned in front of the bridge structure, and the second twin 5in mount is farthest aft. A single 5in mount was located abaft the small aft superstructure. The two shielded quadruple torpedo mounts are also evident. (Yamato Museum)

At the start of the war, the Shiratsuyu class comprised two full and one half destroyer division. Much of the class saw action in the Solomons with one being sunk in 1942 and another two in 1943, both by American surface ships.

The Shiratsuyu class
Total ships in class: 10
Displacement: 1,685 tons standard; 1,980 tons full load
Dimensions: length 353ft (overall); beam 33ft; draft 12ft
Maximum speed: 34kts
Endurance: 6,000nm at 15kts
Crew: 180

THE ASASHIO CLASS

The size of Japanese destroyers kept creeping up, and for the next class no effort was made to adhere to treaty limitations. This decision allowed designers to add another 300 tons of weight and make a longer ship with an increased beam. The result was the Asashio class, which presented a powerful and balanced appearance and was the basis for the next two classes of destroyers. It was, in essence, the standard IJN destroyer with its high speed, powerful torpedo fit, and heavy gun armament.

The torpedo armament remained at two quadruple launchers with eight spare torpedoes. The main gun battery was increased to three twin 5in turrets, one forward and two aft. Power was increased to 50,000shp, and with improved turbines speed was increased to 35kts.

These units saw heavy action from the start of the war and were heavily involved in the Solomons campaign. One was sunk in October 1942 by aircraft off Guadalcanal, and another two were also sunk by aircraft in the Bismarck Sea in March 1943. Another was sunk in 1943 by American surface units.

The Asashio class
Total ships in class: 10
Displacement: 1,961 tons standard; 2,370 tons full load
Dimensions: length 388ft (overall); beam 34ft; draft 12ft
Maximum speed: 35kts
Endurance: 5,700nm at 10kts
Crew: 200

Asashio, lead ship of her class, is shown in this 1937 view. With slight modification, this was the template for the next two classes of Japanese destroyers. Three twin 5in mounts are evident, as are the two quadruple torpedo mounts. *Asashio* was sunk by Allied air attack during the battle of the Bismarck Sea on March 3, 1943. (Yamato Museum)

Isokaze, a unit of the Kagero class, is shown in this 1940 view. Externally, the Kagero class was essentially a repeat of the preceding Asashio class with some refinements in the placement of the forward torpedo mount and its reloads. (Yamato Museum)

THE KAGERO CLASS

The Asashio class was the basis for the next two classes of destroyers, but the Japanese were not entirely happy with it. During trials, defects were noted with the turbines and with the design of the stem and rudder. The Kagero class corrected these. Overall, the Kagero class can be considered the most successful Japanese destroyer design since it achieved the IJN's primary design requirements in speed, range, and firepower and proved successful in service. When compared to American destroyers of the same period, the Kagero class was superior.

Construction of the class began in 1937, which was after the Japanese had withdrawn from the London Naval Treaty. The design of the Kagero class was completed without reference to treaty limitations. Dimensions were the same as the Asashio class, but there were improvements in the engineering plant, stability, and the layout of the torpedo reloads. Main armament remained at two quadruple torpedo mounts with eight reloads and six 5in guns in three twin mounts.

All ships in the class were completed before the war, and the class saw heavy action from the very start of the conflict. The Kageros formed four and a half destroyer divisions assigned to three different destroyer squadrons. The class was committed early to the Solomon campaign and suffered heavily. Eight ships of the class were lost to various causes during the campaign. Of note, *Hamakaze* became the first Japanese destroyer fitted with radar when she received a Type 22 set in late 1942.

Another Solomons campaign veteran was *Tanikaze*. Among other operations, the ship participated in the battle of Kula Gulf. This Kagero-class unit was sunk by submarine attack in June 1944. (Yamato Museum)

Completed too late to take part in the Solomons campaign, Yugumo-class unit *Hamanami* is shown here in October 1943. The position of the Type 22 radar can be seen on the foremast. (Yamato Museum)

The Kagero class
Total ships in class: 19
Displacement: 2,033 tons standard; 2,490 tons full load
Dimensions: length 389ft (overall); beam 35ft; draft 12ft
Maximum speed: 35kts
Endurance: 5,000nm at 18kts
Crew: 240

THE YUGUMO CLASS

The 19-ship Yugumo class represented the epitome of Japanese destroyer design. Construction began in late 1940 but only a few were in commission by the start of the war. These were essentially repeats of the previous Kagero class with only minor changes. Overall displacement was slightly raised, the hull was lengthened, and the bridge was streamlined. Armament also remained the same, but the 5in mounts were of a different type that allowed elevation to 75 degrees.

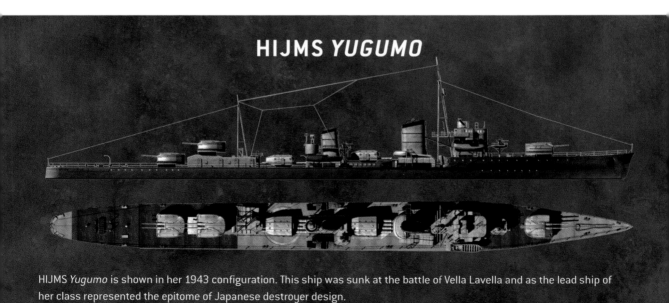

HIJMS *YUGUMO*

HIJMS *Yugumo* is shown in her 1943 configuration. This ship was sunk at the battle of Vella Lavella and as the lead ship of her class represented the epitome of Japanese destroyer design.

As these ships entered service, they formed three destroyer divisions. Seven were lost during the Solomons campaign.

The Yugumo class
Total ships in class: 19
Displacement: 2,077 tons standard; 2,520 tons full load
Dimensions: length 391ft (overall); beam 35ft; draft 12ft
Maximum speed: 35kts
Endurance: 5,000nm at 18kts
Crew: 228

THE AKITSUKI CLASS

The largest Japanese destroyers of the war were the 12 units of the Akitsuki class. These were originally designed to provide antiaircraft protection to carriers and other fleet units. The ship was designed around the new 3.9in high-velocity gun. For the first time, a Japanese destroyer was provided with four twin gun mounts. These guns were successful in service and possessed a high rate of fire and an even longer surface range than the American 5in guns. The offensive potential of the class was increased when a quadruple torpedo mount was added to the design. Four spare torpedoes were also provided.

Construction of this class was begun in late 1941. Of the 12 units eventually completed, only three saw action in the Solomons. Two of these were sunk, one by gunfire and the second by American torpedo boats during a supply run to Guadalcanal.

The Akitsuki class
Total ships in class: 12
Displacement: 2,701 tons standard; 3,700 tons full load
Dimensions: length 440ft (overall); beam 38ft; draft 14ft
Maximum speed: 33kts
Endurance: 8,300nm at 18kts
Crew: 300

The lead ship of the Akitsuki class running sea trials in May 1942. The ship was much larger than the previous classes of Japanese fleet destroyers and featured four twin 3.9in turrets and a single quadruple torpedo mount. (Yamato Museum)

THE COMBATANTS

US NAVY DESTROYER CREWS

Life on any warship is difficult, but on a destroyer it was especially hard. There was no extra room for any designed crew comfort, and the small hull of a destroyer was often lashed about in any kind of sea. In spite of this, life aboard a destroyer can be exhilarating. The most iconic image of a destroyer would be that of its high-speed approach to within a few thousand yards of the enemy to deliver a devastating torpedo attack. The shared hardship, danger, and sheer excitement of destroyer crews made them close. Destroyer crews were small enough that every crewmember could know everybody else and prewar terms of service usually resulted in individuals staying on board the same ship for many years, further contributing to the sense of community. Destroyer crews saw themselves as representative of the "real" Navy with their close connection to the perils of the sea and a required premium on smart seamanship. Unlike in the battleship navy, or even the cruiser navy, there was no time for nonsense like spit and polish aboard a destroyer.

American destroyers were general-purpose platforms able to perform a variety of missions. Though torpedo attacks constituted a prime mission, equally important were general escort and scouting, which required high degrees of gunnery skill against both surface and air targets. Another important mission was screening fleet units from submarine attack. These different missions competed for the limited space in a destroyer hull, as well as for drill time by the crew. In addition to the weapons, sensors, and other equipment required to carry out its varied missions, the ship's power plant was a marvel of engineering that could generate enough power to drive the ship at speeds of over 35kts.

Jammed among the weapons and engineering spaces were the crew. Living space for the crew was usually located aft. Officers' staterooms and the wardroom were usually located amidships or near the bridge. Squeezed into the hull were also crew messing and washing areas, storage for fuel, ammunition, and food, and a small sick bay equipped to handle anything from routine cases to battle casualties. There was no wasted space on a destroyer. The cramped conditions on a destroyer got worse as the war progressed and crew sizes expanded to meet the need for additional gunners to operate the proliferation of antiaircraft guns and the specialists required to maintain and operate the growing numbers of radars and other gear. The spaces were not air conditioned, so conditions in the tropical South Pacific can best be described as difficult. However, morale remained high, especially after the tide began to turn and the Americans commenced their advance up the Solomons. The danger of duty aboard a destroyer was never far from the crew's mind, and respect for their Japanese counterparts remained high.

The officer commanding a destroyer usually held the rank of commander or lieutenant commander. Whatever his rank, he was addressed as "Captain" and he had complete authority over all personnel and operations on the ship. His average age was 30–40 years. All destroyer captains were Naval Academy graduates. The overall caliber of destroyer captains was generally high. Training at Annapolis was technically proficient and provided a homogeneous pool of officers who valued aggression in combat. Perhaps most remarkably and importantly, these same officers possessed an ability to adapt to change, though there were some areas where this proved difficult as has already been discussed. Certainly, from a technical standpoint, American naval officers and crews took quickly to new types of equipment and ideas on how to use them.

A destroyer crew was organized into five departments, each performing one of the primary functions of the ship. The largest department was the Gunnery Department, which was headed by the ship's gunnery officer. He was responsible for the maintenance and operation of all the ship's guns, torpedoes, and antisubmarine gear, as well as all munitions and all fire-control equipment. Most of the ship's officers were assigned to this department. The Navigation Department was responsible for fixing the position of the ship at all times. This department maintained the ship's log and war diary.

The Engineering Department maintained and operated the engineering plant and all other machinery, except electrical equipment. The head of this department was known as the Chief Engineer. The Construction and Repair Department was responsible for ensuring the ship was in proper material condition for combat. The head of the department wore two hats as First Lieutenant responsible for deck operations and Damage Control Officer responsible for damage control training and equipment. The supply officer headed the Supply Department, which had responsibility for administering and acquiring all required supplies, from fuel to food. Each department was organized into a number of divisions, each usually led by a junior officer.

The ship maintained three watch sections. Since the normal duty watch was four hours, the crew's life was built around a four hours on, eight hours off schedule. Of course, the "off" time was not idle time since that was when normal duties had to be

CAPTAIN ARLEIGH ALBERT BURKE USN

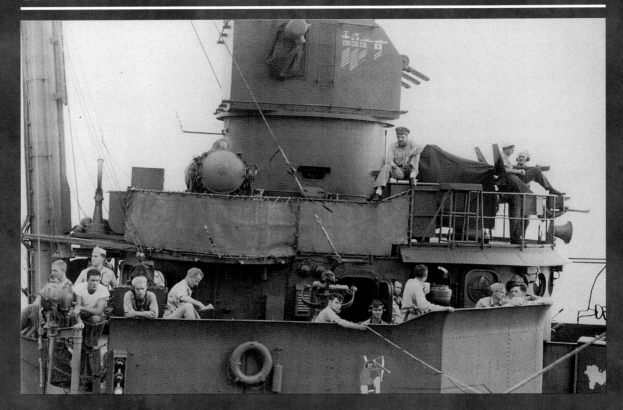

Burke (reading) on the starboard bridge wing of his flagship, *Charles Ausburne*, during operations in the Solomon Islands. The "Little Beaver" insignia of Destroyer Squadron 23 is painted on the ship's bridge wing. Note the scoreboard painted on the side of the Mark 37 fire-control director. (NHHC NH 59854)

Burke was a dedicated destroyer man throughout much of his career. He led the way to developing new destroyer tactics during the Solomons campaign. In his honor, the Navy named its current class of destroyers – today's mainstays of the American surface fleet – after him.

Born in 1901, he gained an appointment to the US Naval Academy despite never having finished high school. After graduating from Annapolis in 1923, he focused on gunnery. Between sea tours, he received a master's degree in chemical engineering. One of his fleet tours was a 1939–40 command of a destroyer, which received many fleet-wide awards for excellence.

At the start of the war in the Pacific, due to his experience with development and procurement of guns, Lieutenant Commander Burke was assigned to the Navy Yard in

Washington, DC as an inspector of newly built gun mounts. It took him until early 1943 to get a combat assignment to the Pacific. He arrived as a destroyer division commander in February 1943. His unit was assigned to the task force under Rear Admiral "Tip" Merrill. Merrill was open to new thinking and soon learned that his destroyer skippers felt unnecessarily restricted by existing tactics. In May, Burke forwarded to Merrill a report titled "Employment of Destroyers" in which Burke stressed the need to exploit surprise and conduct a destroyer torpedo attack first, followed by cruiser gunfire only after the torpedoes had struck their targets. Before Burke had a chance to execute these tactics, he was transferred out of Merrill's command.

Burke continued to refine his plan and as a student of military history, was influenced by the strategy of Roman general Scipio Africanus. Scipio used a strategy of splitting his army into two wings to hit his opponent from different directions. Burke applied this concept to destroyer warfare. In destroyer terms, this called for Burke to divide his force when radar picked up an enemy contact. The first group moved to a position off the enemy's bow and launched a half-salvo of torpedoes. These ships would then conduct a 90-degree turn to avoid any enemy torpedoes fired in response. When the torpedoes of the first group struck, these ships would open fire with guns to finish off any cripples and to distract the enemy. This would allow the second group off the enemy's other bow to conduct a torpedo attack.

In October 1943, Burke was transferred back to Merrill's command and would soon get a chance to try his tactics on the Japanese. On October 23, 1943 Captain Burke broke his broad pennant as the commanding officer of Destroyer Squadron 23 aboard destroyer *Charles Ausburne* in Espiritu Santo. Desron 23, later nicknamed "the Little Beavers" by Burke, was the only destroyer squadron to win a Presidential Unit Citation in World War II. Burke would command Desron 23 from October 23 until March 26, 1944.

Burke quickly laid out his command principles to his destroyer skippers in Desron 23: "SPEED: move quickly while the other fellow is trying to make up his mind. LOOK FOR FIGHTS: if you look for them, you'll probably find them. BE PREPARED: if you're ready for a fight you should win your share." (Cracknell 1971: 201)

Burke was assigned two Destroyer Divisions, 45 and 46, totaling eight Fletcher-class destroyers.

On the eve of his command's first action, he took the opportunity to discuss the upcoming operation and lessons learned from previous actions with his destroyer skippers. This was the same approach taken by British admiral Nelson and his "Band of Brothers."

Burke's first major action was covering the invasion of Bougainville. After the American landings, Burke and Merrill prepared for the Japanese challenge they knew was coming. The Japanese did respond, and Merrill had his hands full with a Japanese force that included two heavy cruisers. Merrill adopted Burke's concepts and decided to let his destroyers play a leading role. They would begin the battle with a torpedo attack, after which Merrill's light cruisers would engage in a gunnery duel beyond the assessed range of Japanese torpedoes.

The battle did not go exactly as scripted, but Merrill and Burke accomplished their mission. Radar picked up the Japanese at 35,900yd allowing Burke to set up Destroyer Division 45 for a torpedo attack on them. The Japanese foiled the attack with a well-timed maneuver. In a confusing night action during which the performance of Burke's destroyers was far from flawless, the Japanese made more mistakes and were forced to withdraw after the loss of a light cruiser and a destroyer. The only major American damage was inflicted by a torpedo that hit the stern of one of Burke's destroyers.

On November 24, Burke picked up his nickname "31-knot Burke" in a message from Halsey. Earlier, Burke had reported to Halsey that he could only make 28kts because of an engineering problem on one of his destroyers. The ship was able to increase its speed to 31kts – a point cheekily acknowledged by Halsey when reported by Burke. On November 25, Burke fought the battle of Cape St. George, his most memorable action. Burke closed out the war as Chief of Staff for Admiral Marc Mitscher, commander of the Pacific Fleet's carrier striking force. After the war, Burke held many important posts, including Chief of Naval Operations for six years.

Officers of Destroyer Squadron 23 ashore at Purvis Bay, Solomon Islands, on May 24, 1944. Present are Burke and the five skippers of the destroyers that participated in the battle of Cape St. George. Pictured, left to right, are Commander R.A. Gano, Commanding Officer, USS *Dyson*; Commander Luther K. Reynolds, Commanding Officer, USS *Charles Ausburne*; Captain Arleigh A. Burke, Squadron Commodore; Commander B.L. Austin, Commander, Destroyer Division 46; Commander D.C. Hamberger, Commanding Officer, USS *Converse*; Commander Herald Stout, Commanding Officer, USS *Claxton*; and Commander Henry J. Armstrong, Commanding Officer, USS *Spence*. (NHHC NH 59864)

performed. In addition to a watch section, every member of the crew (except the Captain and the executive officer) was also assigned a General Quarters station that was to be occupied during battle.

The level of training and education of the US Navy's sailors going into the war was quite high. It is important to note that conscription for the Navy did not begin until December 1942. This meant that all destroyer crews going into the war were composed of volunteers, many of whom had served considerable time together.

IJN DESTROYER CREWS

Since the IJN was locked into an inferior position relative to the US Navy by a number of naval treaties and by the economic reality that Japan could never match the US Navy in a numerical sense, intensive and realistic training was seen by the Japanese as one of the potential great equalizers. When added to the moral superiority the Japanese thought they possessed and the fact that each Japanese ship was designed to be bigger, faster, and more powerful than its American counterpart, the IJN felt it had every chance of overcoming the numerically superior Americans and winning a war at sea.

An essential building block of this belief was the concept of making training so intense that it could never be surpassed by the Americans. As has already been discussed, IJN doctrine for surface combat was already in place, and though the entire decisive battle precept did not translate well into the Pacific War, the emphasis on small unit tactics did. To make these tactics second nature to the units that had to conduct them under the fog and stress of actual combat, constant and rigorous exercising was required. The Combined Fleet's commander in the 1920s ordered the fleet to engage in night-combat exercises "more heroic than under actual battle conditions" (Marder 1981: 292). The fact that this was not mere rhetoric was confirmed in August 1927 during night torpedo exercises. Off northwestern Honshu, during a torpedo exercise on a dark night, destroyers were moving into a favorable position for a torpedo attack when two of them collided with light cruisers. The results of the high-speed collisions were catastrophic. The Momi-class destroyer *Warabi* was cut in two by *Jinstu* and sank with 104 casualties. Destroyer *Ashi* was heavily damaged colliding with *Naka* with 29 more casualties. Training was often conducted in the Northern Pacific under severe weather and sea conditions.

The IJN's training year began on December 1 and started with single-ship and squadron-level training through April. This transitioned into training with the entire Combined Fleet in May, which did not end until October. Combat conditions were replicated during training to the fullest extent possible. The rigor of these exercises was such that Japanese officers described them as tougher than actual combat. During the height of the training season, the pace was relentless and reduced shore leave to two or three successive days each month. Another training edge enjoyed by the Japanese was the fact that after 1937 ships and crews were exposed to actual combat conditions off the Chinese coast.

Destroyer crews were well drilled in battle tactics and execution. A well-trained crew could gain a bearing on a torpedo target and launch a full torpedo broadside within a couple of minutes of getting a sighting report from an alert lookout. Another key skill was reloading torpedoes, which a well-drilled crew could accomplish within a 15–20-minute period. This is how a former destroyer captain described his crew's training regimen:

> In my training plan, the first month was devoted to shipboard fundamentals … If a drill fell short of my standard, I personally demonstrated and directed its rehearsal, dozens of times if necessary. I drummed it into the men that, in a life-and-death struggle, nothing short of perfection is adequate. At first they were bewildered by such high standard. But gradually they became willing and eager to carry out my orders. (Hara n.d.: 163–64)

The quality of personnel aboard a destroyer was outstanding, at least in the first part of the war. The average Japanese naval officer was highly intelligent, brave, and loyal. All destroyer officers entered service through the Naval Academy located on the island of Etajima near Hiroshima. Etajima had its pick of the finest young men in the nation, as evidenced in 1937 when over 7,100 applicants contended for 240 places. Academy life was focused on building discipline, toughness, and fitness and included physical abuse, setting the tone for the entire navy where beatings were all too commonplace. The quality of instruction at Etajima was generally good, but new officers were also noted for a lack of assertiveness and independent judgment, and an inability to see beyond narrow tactical concerns. This was an aftermath of an education system that valued conformity. In action, this translated into an occasional lack of aggression because of the inability to foresee and act decisively in unexpected circumstances.

On balance, the IJN's personnel system produced a small, highly trained cadre of career officers and men. This strategy resulted in a high-caliber force manned by extraordinarily well-trained, motivated, disciplined, and experienced crews. On average, the state of training aboard a Japanese destroyer was superior to that of an American destroyer. In the early stages of the war, and in the night battles around Guadalcanal, this superiority mattered. Later in the war, under the strain of heavy losses, this strategy was totally insufficient. The quality of Japanese destroyer crews, along with that of the rest of the IJN, could not be maintained.

CAPTAIN HARA TAMEICHI IJN

Hara is certainly the best-known Japanese destroyer captain of the war. This is not necessarily because he was the finest captain of the war, although he was arguably among the best, but because he wrote a book — translated into English after the war — based on his experiences. Hara was typical of the well-trained and dedicated Japanese destroyer commanders of the war. His success was undeniable and was demonstrated by the fact that the losses of his crews throughout the war was lower than any other Japanese commander with equivalent combat experience.

Hara was born in 1900 and went to Etajima in 1918. He graduated three years later as 40th out of a class of 150. He quickly showed his maverick side, stating his distaste for Etajima since he despised the physical brutality that was an accepted part of the culture. After graduation, he did a brief tour on the old armored cruiser *Kasuga* before being assigned to his first destroyer, the small, third-rate *Hatsuyuki*. In Hara's day, the top Etajima graduates were earmarked for staff duty, the second tier were sent to battleship and cruiser assignments, and the third tier were relegated to destroyer duty. Hara blossomed in the destroyer community. He served aboard two more destroyers before taking the advanced course at the Destroyer School at Yokosuka, which set him up as a future destroyer skipper. After completing this course, he was assigned as the chief torpedo officer aboard three destroyers, the last of which was the Special Type destroyer *Fubuki*. In these capacities, he spent time studying and trying to understand why existing Japanese torpedo doctrine resulted in so few hits during torpedo drills. His conclusion, which he was able to prove mathematically, was that the doctrine was flawed. He revised the doctrine and improved torpedo marksmanship throughout the fleet. This was no mean feat, and showed his outstanding technical abilities and willingness to take on authority.

In 1933, Hara was promoted to lieutenant commander and during the next year given his first command, the destroyer *Nagatsuki*. By 1937, he was given command of Special Type destroyer *Amagiri*. Just before the war, he was transferred to take over the new *Amatsukaze*. As one of the Kagero class, this was among Japan's most powerful destroyers. *Amatsukaze* was assigned to Destroyer Squadron 2, Destroyer Division 16 and was very active during the first stage of the war. Destroyer Squadron 2 was assigned to cover the invasion of the Philippines and later the invasion of the Dutch East Indies. *Amatsukaze* took part in the battle of the Java Sea in February 1942, where the massive torpedo attacks launched by Japanese destroyers proved ineffective.

Hara's *Amatsukaze* was one of the more famous and successful units of the Kagero class. She was fitted with experimental high-pressure boilers. She was sunk by air attack in April 1945. (Yamato Museum)

Hara was also present at Midway where he escorted the invasion convoy. When the IJN was forced to head into the South Pacific to respond to the American invasion of Guadalcanal, Hara's ship took part in the two carrier battles of the campaign in August and October. Finally, in November, Hara got a chance to do what he had trained for his entire career. In the first naval battle of Guadalcanal, *Amatsukaze* found herself in the thick of this intense, point-blank night action. Hara engaged the American destroyer *Barton* and sank her with torpedoes. He had a close torpedo shot against cruiser *San Francisco*, but fired four torpedoes at such a close range they could not arm before hitting the target. He raked the cruiser with gunfire. While Hara was doing this, light cruiser *Helena* shattered *Amatsukaze* with 6in gunfire, shredding Hara's command and killing 43. Hara was able to bring his badly battered destroyer back to Truk.

After Guadalcanal, Hara was assigned to assume command of Destroyer Division 27. This prospect initially appalled him since the unit had a bad reputation and was comprised of old Shiratsuyu-class ships. Hara's flagship was the destroyer *Shigure*, and it was on this ship that Hara made his name. The ship went through eight months of action from Truk and Rabaul, and engaged in several battles described in this book, as well as other transport runs,

escort missions, and air raids, and never lost a man. This made *Shigure* the most famous destroyer in the fleet and she became known as the "Indestructible Destroyer."

After relinquishing command of his destroyer division, which had ceased to exist after losses and required overhauls, Hara was assigned ashore at the Torpedo School. He languished there until December 1944 when he was assigned as commanding officer of the light cruiser *Yahagi*, one of the few large units still active in the Imperial Fleet. *Yahagi* was assigned to escort superbattleship *Yamato* on her suicidal run to Okinawa in April 1945. Despite the crew's confidence in their famous captain, *Yahagi* was blown apart by air-launched bombs and torpedoes and 446 of the crew were killed.

The picture that Hara paints of himself in his book is that of an impatient officer who was always right. He was unmercifully critical of his senior officers, not just after the war, but during it as well. Unquestionably, he was a capable destroyer leader, possessing a combination of technical skill, aggression, and somewhat uniquely for a fairly junior Japanese officer, an ability to carefully consider the reasons behind an operation. It would be incorrect to say he was a typical Japanese naval officer, but he typified the capable commanders of the IJN's destroyers.

COMBAT

PRELIMINARIES

The Americans landed on the islands of Rendova and New Georgia on June 30. This first American encroachment into the Central Solomons began a series of clashes that would last until November 1943. After two unsuccessful attempts to attack the landing areas, the IJN reverted to using its destroyers as transports to reinforce the garrisons on these and nearby islands. The first attempt on July 5 to land troops on Kolombangara Island was thwarted by the presence of a large American force in Kula Gulf. The following night, the Japanese tried again with a total of ten destroyers organized into three divisions. Two divisions were carrying troops and supplies and the third division with three destroyers was assigned as a covering force. The Americans countered with a force of three light cruisers and four destroyers under Rear Admiral W. Ainsworth. Ainsworth was relying on the fast-firing 6in guns aboard his cruisers as his primary offensive punch. His plan called for the cruisers to engage at 8,000–10,000yd, which he believed was beyond the range of Japanese torpedoes. Once the cruisers had opened up, the destroyers would engage with torpedoes, primarily to finish off the Japanese ships crippled by gunfire. This plan was obviously flawed since it was ignorant of the true capabilities of the Type 93 torpedo and condemned the American destroyers to a totally supporting role.

The ensuing battle of Kula Gulf, fought at night in the early hours of July 6, went pretty much according to script. With the aid of radar, the American cruisers opened the battle with gunfire at 7,000yd, but focused their fire on the lead Japanese destroyer

Niizuki. Within seconds, the other two destroyers of the covering force fired a torpedo broadside at the gun flashes of the cruisers. Three torpedoes struck the light cruiser *Helena*, which quickly sank. Another cruiser was hit by a torpedo, but it proved to be a dud. No further American ships were damaged; gunfire damaged another five of the Japanese destroyers and another ran aground and was destroyed by aircraft the next day. Ainsworth had failed to stop the Japanese from delivering reinforcements and had lost more tonnage than the Japanese.

A week later, another clash took place off Kolombangara where the Japanese were attempting to land additional troops. In the battle of Kolombangara on July 13, an Allied force under Ainsworth of two American light cruisers and a New Zealand light cruiser, supported by ten destroyers, faced a smaller Japanese force of one light cruiser and five destroyers. Both sides received advance warning of the other's approach from friendly seaplanes. The Japanese were the first to attack, launching 22 Type 93s from the destroyers and another seven torpedoes from light cruiser *Jinstu*. Minutes later, four American destroyers in the lead group placed 21 torpedoes in the water, but since they were launched at 10,000–11,000yd, all were ineffective. Another three destroyers in the rear group launched 17 more torpedoes. The cruisers opened fire at *Jinstu*, due to her being the biggest radar target and also because she had used her searchlight. The cruiser was quickly hit in her bridge and engine room and came to a halt, burning fiercely.

When the initial Japanese torpedo barrage reached Ainsworth's force, only one struck home on the New Zealand cruiser *Leander*. Leaving two destroyers to assist *Leander*, Ainsworth sent the rest of his force to chase the fleeing Japanese. The Japanese were not fleeing, but seeking to gain time to reload their torpedo tubes. Once accomplished, four Japanese destroyers headed southeast to engage the approaching Americans. The Japanese succeeded in firing a second barrage of torpedoes before the Americans could decide which radar contacts were friendly or enemy. The light cruisers *Honolulu* and *St. Louis* were both struck by a torpedo forward and lost their bows. A destroyer was also struck by a torpedo and was later scuttled. After this battle, with all three cruisers torpedoed, most American commanders realized that using their cruisers to chase Japanese destroyers in the restricted waters of the Solomons was not the best strategy. From now on, it would be up to the destroyers to carry the burden against the IJN's destroyers still intent on reinforcing the various Japanese garrisons.

LEFT Light cruiser *Helena* firing her 6in battery at the battle of Kula Gulf. Minutes later, the ship was torpedoed and sunk. Astern of *Helena* is light cruiser *St. Louis*. Both are using flashless powder, but as is evident from this photograph, using the main guns still provided a signature for Japanese destroyers to target with torpedoes. (NHHC 80-G-54553)

RIGHT A Japanese ship, almost certainly destroyer *Niizuki*, burning during the battle of Kula Gulf as seen from destroyer *Nicholas*. As often happened during night battles using radar-controlled gunnery, the Americans focused their gunfire on a single ship, thereby allowing other Japanese ships to escape and prepare retaliatory torpedo attacks. (NHHC 80-G-52851)

At the battle of Kolombangara, the Japanese succeeded in torpedoing all three Allied cruisers present. *Honolulu*, shown here, had her bow blown off. Another Type 93 torpedo hit her astern, but failed to explode. (NHHC 80-G-259422)

The first American destroyer leader to best his Japanese counterpart was Commander Frederick Moosbrugger. He is shown here after being decorated with the Navy Cross on September 10, 1943 following his victory at the battle of Vella Gulf. (Naval Heritage and History Command (NHHC) 80-G-84005)

THE BATTLE OF VELLA GULF

In the aftermath of their victory on July 13, the Japanese conducted another reinforcement run into the Kula Gulf on July 19, supported by heavy cruisers. After this attempt to draw the Americans into a major engagement failed, the Japanese decided that the direct route to Vila on the southern tip of Kolombangara was too risky. Future runs would go through the Vella Gulf on the western side of Kolombangara. Two runs were conducted using this route on July 22 and August 1.

The Americans were prepared to contest the next Japanese reinforcement run into the Vella Gulf. There had been a turnover of leadership of the American surface forces and the new commander, Rear Admiral Theodore Wilkinson, was prepared to entertain new ideas and new tactics. Leading the way was Commander Arleigh Burke, a destroyer division commander. Though he was temporarily reassigned before the next skirmish occurred, his new tactics would be implemented in a modified form. The officer in charge of the next American attempt to derail the Tokyo Express was Commander Frederick Moosbrugger, commander of Destroyer Division 12. Moosbrugger was not convinced that American torpedoes and torpedo tactics were worthless. He convinced Wilkinson that he be allowed to build his battle plan on a radar-guided night torpedo attack. Under his command were the three destroyers of his division and three more from Destroyer Division 15 under Commander Rodger Simpson.

The plan called for the American force to operate in two independent units. After gaining radar contact with the enemy,

Mahan-class destroyer *Dunlap* shown in May 1942. Her No. 3 5in gun has already been removed. *Dunlap* was Moosbrugger's flagship at the battle of Vella Gulf. (NHHC 19-N-30007)

Moosbrugger's force would launch torpedoes while Simpson's group prepared to engage with gunfire after the torpedoes struck. The plan was a modified version of Burke's concepts and represented a radical departure on two accounts. First, it called for the forces to be divided, which violated the age-old principle of concentration of force and in a night action, increased the problems of identification of friendly ships. Most importantly, it placed the torpedo as the primary offensive weapon of choice. Based on the performance of American destroyers and their torpedoes to date, it was a bold move. Before the battle, Moosbrugger had the opportunity to review the operation with Simpson and the commanding officers of the six destroyers.

The Japanese were employing a plan that had worked in earlier runs. Their force of four destroyers would move to the north of Bougainville, enter the Slot through the Bougainville Strait between the Bougainville and Choiseul Islands, and approach Kolombangara from the west, entering Vella Gulf before moving through the Blackett Strait where troops and supplies would be loaded into barges for final movement to Vila. For this operation, the Japanese employed four destroyers, three from Destroyer Division 4 under Captain Sugiura Kaju and a fourth from Destroyer Division 27 under Captain Hara Tameichi. In a pre-departure conference, Hara warned that to repeat the operation was courting disaster.

The battle of Vella Gulf, August 6–7, 1943
American forces
Destroyer Division 12 (Commander Moosbrugger on *Dunlap*): *Dunlap* (Mahan class); *Craven* (Gridley class); *Maury* (Gridley class)
Destroyer Division 15 (Commander Simpson on *Lang*): *Lang* (Benham class); *Sterett* (Benham class); *Stack* (Benham class)
Japanese forces
Destroyer Division 4 (Captain Sugiura Kaju on *Hagikaze*): *Hagikaze* (Kagero class); *Arashi* (Kagero class); *Kawakaze* (Shiratsuyu class)
Destroyer Division 27 (Captain Hara Tameichi on *Shigure*): *Shigure* (Shiratsuyu class)

Benham-class destroyer *Stack* pictured in March 1943. *Stack* was present at the battle of Vella Gulf where as a member of Destroyer Division 46, she finished off the three Japanese destroyers torpedoed earlier in the battle. (NHHC 19-N-42249)

Late on August 6, both sides were entering Vella Gulf. The Americans knew that a Japanese operation was in process and the Japanese commander also assumed that a night engagement was possible since he had been sighted by aircraft earlier in the day. The Japanese entered Vella Gulf from the north in a compact column with *Hagikaze* in the lead. According to plan, the American force entered from the south in two columns with Moosbrugger's ships in the lead. The sea was calm, but with no moon, it was a very dark night.

At 2333hrs, the SG radar on Moosbrugger's flagship gained contact on the approaching Japanese. The range was 19,700yd. On this occasion, American electronics were better than Japanese optics. This could be explained by the fact that Kolombangara Island was behind the Americans, allowing them to blend in on this dark night. With the Japanese apparently oblivious to any danger, Moosbrugger put his plan into motion. Soon, the radar contact was better defined as four separate contacts giving the Americans a better idea of what they were facing. Moosbrugger ordered his three ships to fire torpedoes to port against the approaching Japanese. Simpson's ships, sailing to the starboard side of Moosbrugger's column, were ordered to swing behind and then cross the Japanese "T" to be prepared to engage with guns. Moosbrugger had the luxury of allowing the Japanese to close his port bow to some 6,300yd before ordering his torpedo attack. At 2341hrs, 22 torpedoes left their mounts for an expected four and a half minute run to their targets.

After launching his weapons, Moosbrugger ordered his ships to turn away from the Japanese; this would present as small a target as possible for any returning Japanese torpedoes. Too late did Japanese lookouts spot the American destroyers against the dark mass of Kolombangara. By the time the Japanese sighted torpedo wakes, disaster was only seconds away. A young officer aboard destroyer *Maury* described the tension as the Americans waited for the torpedoes to reach their targets:

Captain Sims had moved back to the port wing where he braced himself, one arm around the voice-tube, the other hugging the pelorus, and his head thrust forward, eyes trying to pierce the dark… Every eye topsides strained to penetrate the night …

"Mark first fish!" I shouted up the voice-tube – nothing!

The silence screamed!

"Mark two!" – five seconds passed, then a great tower of orange flame leapt into the sky. From the bridge they could see three ships to the right of the flame. "Explosion on port quarter" was the laconic report from a lookout. "We hit her!" the captain shouted into the voice-tube …

"Mark three!" – nothing.

"Mark four!" – two seconds – a second tower of flame rose to match the first.

"Huge explosion! Different ship!" the captain shouted down the voice-tube. Shock waves from the explosions shook the whole ship.

"Mark five" – a moment's pause – "Big explosion!"

"Mark six!" – "Tall column of fire! That is a different ship!"

"Mark seven!" – three seconds – "Huge column of fire to the right!"

"Mark eight!" – nothing. (Crenshaw 1998: 212)

Starting at 2345hrs, calamity engulfed the Japanese force. The lead ship, *Hagikaze*, was the first to be struck by torpedoes. Two struck; the second aft in the engine room, which brought her to a stop. The next ship, *Arashi*, was also hit by two torpedoes, which also destroyed her engineering spaces. The third ship, *Kawakaze*, was struck by a single torpedo under the bridge, which detonated a magazine and caused a huge fire. *Shigure* was the last ship in line. After sighting the torpedoes, Hara ordered a hard starboard turn and a full eight-torpedo broadside loosed off against the Americans located off his port side. As described by Hara, *Shigure* escaped by the narrowest of margins:

As the eighth torpedo was about to be released I caught sight of telltale white torpedo tracks fanning out in our direction, the nearest within 800 meters [875yd]. I shouted again for hard starboard helm. In the same moment I saw a pillar of fire shoot up from amidships of *Arashi*, and two from *Kawakaze*. Lead ship *Hagikaze* was beyond and in line with the two victims so that I could not see her.

Looking again at the water, I held my breath. Three torpedoes were streaking toward *Shigure*'s bow, which was swinging rapidly to the right.

My knees almost gave in as I clutched the handrail. The first torpedo passed 20 meters [22yd] ahead of the bow, the second was closer, and the third appeared certain to hit. It did not, however, or if it did it was just a glancing blow on the skin of the rapidly turning ship. I thought I felt a dull thud from aft but could not be sure. Looking around again I saw several torpedoes running 30 meters [33yd] or more in front of the bow, as the ship was completing a full circle in its desperate evasion turn… Those two minutes just passed were the most breath-taking ones of my life. (Hara n.d.: 177)

In fact, Hara's escape was closer than he knew. When *Shigure* was drydocked, it was discovered that the thud he thought he felt was a hit on the ship's rudder, which caused a hole but did not explode. After dodging the American torpedo barrage, *Shigure* started to make smoke and moved to the northwest at high speed to reload her torpedo tubes.

The opening seconds of the battle brought victory for the Americans. Of the 22 torpedoes launched, at least five had hit accounting for three destroyers; *Shigure* had barely escaped, making it a clean sweep for Moosbrugger. Now all that remained

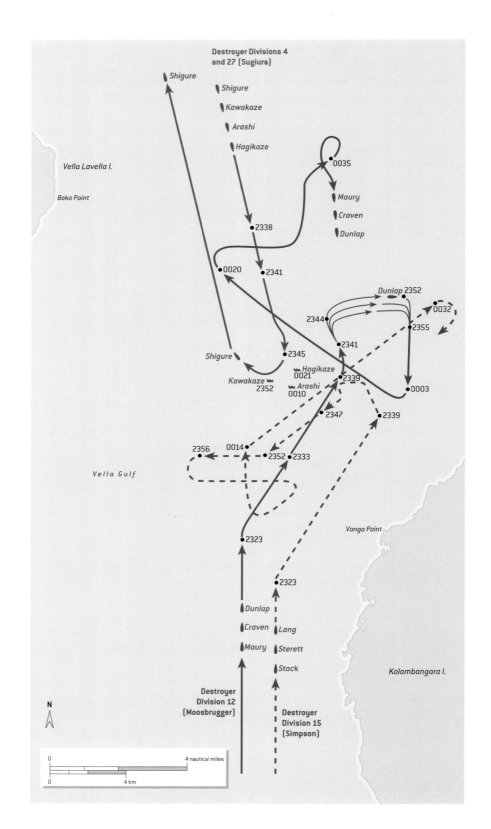

Destroyer Divisions 4
and 27 (Sugiura)

Shigure

Shigure

Kawakaze

Arashi

Hagikaze

0035

Maury

Craven

Dunlap

Vella Lavella I.

Boko Point

2338

0020 2341

Dunlap 2352

2344 0032

2355

2341

2345 2339

Hagikaze 0003

Shigure 0021

Kawakaze ⚓ *Arashi*

2352 0010

2347 2339

2356 0014 2352 2333

Vella Gulf

2323

Vanga Point

2323

Dunlap

Craven *Lang*

Maury *Sterett*

Stack

Kolombangara I.

Destroyer
Division 12
(Moosbrugger)

Destroyer
Division 15
(Simpson)

N

0			4 nautical miles

0		4 km

The battle of Vella Gulf, August

6–7, 1943.

was to finish off the cripples. At 2347hrs, Simpson's division engaged the burning Japanese ships with their 5in guns. Their first target was *Kawakaze*, now only some 3,000yd to the northwest. The gunfire was intense and deadly, and destroyer *Stack* added to the proceedings with four torpedoes. *Kawakaze* sank at 2352hrs.

Arashi and *Hagikaze* did not survive much longer. Sporadic Japanese gunfire was ineffective, and now both divisions of American ships were concentrating fire on the two burning Japanese wrecks. At 0010hrs, *Arashi*'s magazine blew up. *Hagikaze* proved tough to sink, so at 0021hrs each of Simpson's three destroyers fired another two torpedoes. Three were heard to detonate and *Hagikaze* disappeared.

Hara on *Shigure* briefly gave thoughts of re-engaging, but after realizing that the other three Japanese ships were sunk or out of action, Hara decided to return to Rabaul. For the first time in the war, IJN destroyers had been beaten in a night battle.

THE BATTLE OFF HORANIU

By the time of the next destroyer action, the situation in the Central Solomons had changed. Instead of attacking Kolombangara, which was now strongly garrisoned, Wilkinson instead landed on lightly defended Vella Lavella Island, thus bypassing

The battle off Horaniu, August 18, 1943.

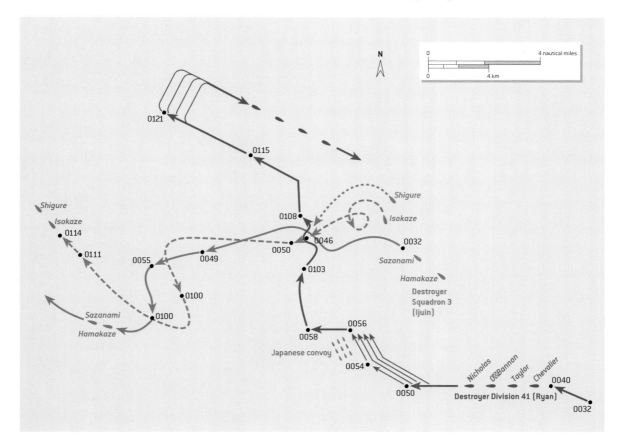

Kolombangara. Unable to contest the landing directly, the Japanese decided to land troops at Horaniu on the northeastern part of Vella Lavella Island in order to maintain a line of communication with the garrison on Kolombangara. With this new base, small craft would be used to supply the garrison instead of destroyers.

On August 17, Destroyer Division 3, under the command of Rear Admiral Ijuin Matsuji, departed Rabaul. The flotilla of small craft that the destroyers were assigned to escort departed the same day from the anchorage at Buin south of Bougainville. When air reconnaissance reported the Japanese convoy, Wilkinson ordered Destroyer Division 41 under Captain Ryan to intercept.

This prewar shot in 1941 shows Kagero-class unit *Hagikaze*. This ship was the flagship of the Japanese force at the battle of Vella Gulf. She did not initially sink after being struck by two torpedoes, but was later dispatched by additional gunfire and torpedo attack and 178 of her crew were killed. (Yamato Museum)

Three of Destroyer Squadron 21's ships under way in the Solomon Islands on August 15, 1943. *O'Bannon* leads the column followed by *Chevalier* and *Taylor*. The ships were photographed from *Nicholas* while en route to the landings at Vella Lavella. (NHHC 80-G-58800)

The battle off Horaniu, August 18, 1943

American forces

Destroyer Division 41 (Captain T.J. Ryan on *Nicholas*): *Nicholas* (Fletcher class); *O'Bannon* (Fletcher class); *Chevalier* (Fletcher class); *Taylor* (Fletcher class)

Japanese forces

Destroyer Squadron 3 (Rear Admiral Ijuin Matsuji on *Sazanami*):

Destroyer Division 17 (Captain Miyazaki Toshio on *Sazanami*): *Sazanami* (Fubuki class); *Hamakaze* (Kagero class); *Isokaze* (Kagero class)

Destroyer Division 27 (Captain Hara Tameichi on *Shigure*): *Shigure* (Shiratsuyu class)

Both commanders knew that an opposing destroyer force was at sea from friendly air reconnaissance. First contact came at 0027hrs when the radar aboard *O'Bannon* reported enemy ships to the northwest at 23,000yd range. At 0032hrs, lookouts aboard *Sazanami* spotted the American force at a range of 16,400yd to the southeast.

Ijuin was in a tactical bind. As he had told his commanders before leaving Rabaul, his primary mission was to protect the convoy, not seek an engagement. This convoy was now located some 16 miles short of its destination at Horaniu, but was situated between the opposing destroyer forces. As Ijuin told Hara after the battle, "I was positive that the enemy, overconfident after his phenomenal August 6 victory, had decided to ignore the vulnerable unescorted convoy, and challenge us to a duel. I headed north to lure the enemy into battle at a safe distance from the convoy." (Hara n.d.: 186) He kept his flagship and *Hamakaze* near the convoy and ordered the other two ships to the north. For his part, Ryan wanted to repeat the previous American success at Vella Gulf and maneuvered his force for a surprise torpedo attack. This was rendered impossible when at 0040hrs a Japanese floatplane dropped a flare over the American force. Since surprise was now impossible, Ryan turned to engage the barges, which were located to his east.

Ijuin responded to the apparent threat to the convoy by ordering a torpedo attack on the Americans. Beginning at 0046hrs, each of his four destroyers launched their weapons until 31 torpedoes were headed toward the Americans at a range of approximately 12,500yd. This attack was thwarted by Ryan's order at 0050hrs to turn to the northwest and another turn at 0054hrs. All of the torpedoes missed.

The Japanese followed their torpedo attack with a gunnery attack beginning at 0057hrs. The American ships were silhouetted in front of a full moon, and the Japanese had capped the American "T." However, their gunnery was ineffective since they possessed no radar and were unwilling to use their searchlights for fear of revealing their position to the Americans. The Japanese hit nothing.

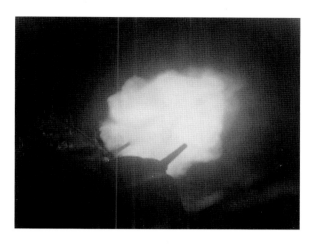

Nicholas firing her forward 5in guns at Japanese destroyers during the battle off Horaniu on August 18, 1943. During this engagement, the Americans fired 3,028 5in rounds from four destroyers inflicting only light damage on two Japanese ships. This demonstrated that even with radar it was very difficult to hit a fast, maneuvering target. (NHHC 80-G-58874)

Ryan had now turned his force to the north to close the Japanese. A gunnery duel ensued between the two sides. Even with the aid of radar, it was difficult for the Americans to hit a frantically moving target that was making smoke to make visual observation more difficult. This is how Hara described the American barrage:

> The next moment, *Shigure* was straddled by enemy shells which fell 20–40 meters [22–44yd] from the ship, kicking up pillars of water and spray. Another barrage, seconds later, bracketed our ship even more closely; and the third just barely missed us.
>
> I craned my neck, and strained my eyes for gun flashes, which simply did not appear. I realized now that we were confronted with the enemy's new flashless powder we had all heard rumors about. That, combined with his radar-controlled guns, presented a formidable opposition. Forgetting my own plans for a torpedo attack, I ordered smoke and a zigzag course.
>
> *Shigure* weaved back and forth through the thickening smoke screen at her full 30kts. But no matter which way we turned shells kept falling around us every six or seven seconds with breath-taking, uncanny tempo. Tension rose as we realized that any moment might bring a direct hit. (Hara n.d.: 188)

At 0100hrs, a near miss landed close to *Hamakaze*. Minutes before, *Chevalier* had launched four torpedoes at a range of 9,000yd with no effect. As the Japanese moved to the northwest, the range increased. The Americans continued to lay down a barrage on the Japanese, and a 5in shell hit *Isokaze* but did not affect her speed. *Shigure* and *Isokaze* fired additional torpedoes at the Americans, but again no hits were scored. Ijuin decided to break off the engagement when the radar room aboard *Hamakaze* reported a large enemy force approaching – a mistaken reference to the Japanese small craft convoy. Ryan did not pursue for long. At 0121hrs, he decided to break off the pursuit to look for the convoy now located to his southeast.

The four destroyers were unable to find any of the small targets until 30 minutes later and were only able to sink a single barge and two submarine chasers. The rest of the convoy's 13 barges, three motor boats, and six escorts were able to reach the safety of the coast of Vella Lavella Island and arrived at Horaniu the next night.

THE BATTLE OF VELLA LAVELLA

Having decided to abandon the Central Solomons, the Japanese proceeded to evacuate the garrison on Kolombangara commencing on September 20. The operation was primarily conducted by barge. On September 30, Ijuin's destroyers failed to engage an American destroyer force because a barge force was positioned between the two destroyer forces. A few days later, Ijuin returned with nine destroyers to evacuate troops off Kolombangara on the night of October 2–3. Six American destroyers were deployed to prevent the evacuation. In a confusing action in which the Japanese believed they were facing four cruisers and three destroyers, no damage was inflicted by either side despite a flurry of torpedoes fired by both sides followed by an exchange of gunfire. The four Japanese destroyers assigned to evacuate soldiers accomplished their mission. Unable to stop the evacuation by the destroyers, the Americans again returned to focus on a Japanese barge convoy, but succeeded in sinking only five of the small craft. The largely successful evacuation of Kolombangara set the stage for the next destroyer clash.

Ijuin was ordered to conduct the evacuation of the Japanese garrison on Vella Lavella Island, the last garrison in the Central Solomons. For this operation, he committed nine destroyers. These were divided into several groups in the hopes of deceiving the Americans about the strength and intentions of the Japanese force. Ijuin exercised direct command of the four most modern destroyers, and gave Hara command of the group consisting of two older destroyers. Three destroyer transports were assigned to accompany a convoy of 12 assorted smaller craft. The Japanese destroyers left Rabaul on the morning of October 6. The convoy of smaller craft left Buin that afternoon.

To contest the Japanese operation, Wilkinson had only a single destroyer division of three ships available. As reinforcements, he detached another destroyer division with three ships from convoy duty and sent them north at high speed to rendezvous at a point northwest off Vella Lavella; however, they were too late for the action and thus Captain Walker's division fought the battle against superior numbers.

The battle of Vella Lavella, October 6, 1943
American forces

Destroyer Squadron 4 (Captain F. Walker on *Selfridge*): *Selfridge* (Porter class); *O'Bannon* (Fletcher class); *Chevalier* (Fletcher class)

Japanese forces

Destroyer Squadron 3 (Rear Admiral Ijuin Matsuji on *Akigumo*):

Destroyer Division 10 (Captain Amano Shigetaka on *Akigumo*): *Akigumo* (Kagero class); *Yugumo* (Yugumo class); *Isokaze* (Kagero class); *Kazegumo* (Yugumo class)

Destroyer Division 27 (Captain Hara Tameichi on *Shigure*): *Shigure* (Shiratsuyu class); *Samidare* (Shiratsuyu class)

Fumizuki, *Matsukaze*, and *Yunagi* were also involved as destroyer transports

As soon as Ijuin's force left Rabaul, it was spotted by American aircraft. Ijuin pressed ahead with his four destroyers and ordered the others to rendezvous with the convoy and proceed to the pick-up point on the northwestern shore of Vella Lavella. On this occasion, Japanese optics proved superior to American electronics. Approaching the pick-up point, Japanese lookouts on Ijuin's force spotted what they

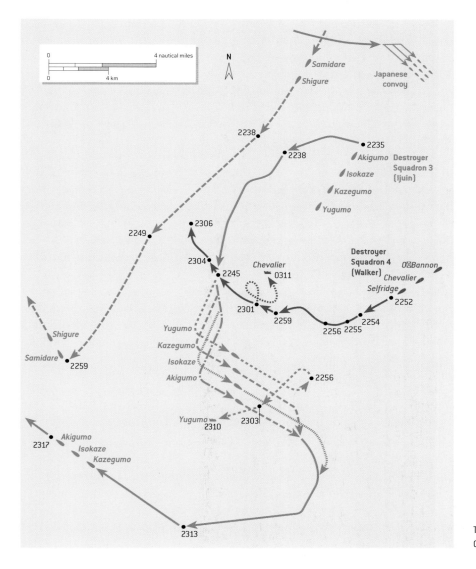

The battle of Vella Lavella, October 6, 1943.

reported as four American destroyers. The contact was quickly lost in a squall, but the alert lookouts had saved the Japanese from another ambush. The entire complexion of the battle changed when Ijuin received word that superior American forces, including cruisers, were present in the area. In response to this faulty information, he ordered his destroyers and the two under Hara to head north just after 2200hrs.

At 2231hrs American radar screens came alive with the detection of the three transport destroyers located to the northwest. Walker ordered his ships to the west, and the SG radars began to pick up more contacts. Walker was not fazed by the aircraft sighting reports that as many as nine Japanese destroyers could be in the area and the fact that his promised reinforcements had not responded to radio calls.

Ijuin changed course to the west at 2235hrs to join with Hara's two destroyers. No sooner than this was done, lookouts on *Kazegumo* reported possible contacts to the east. As Ijuin joined with Hara and now headed to the southwest either to draw the Americans away from the convoy or to gain a better angle for a torpedo attack, Walker was tracking both Japanese groups on radar. Walker intended to engage the larger group with torpedoes while Ijuin, still concerned that he was facing cruisers, planned to launch his torpedoes at long range before his ships were deluged with radar-controlled gunfire. The Americans got their torpedoes off first when at 2254hrs each destroyer launched half of their available weapons, a total of 14 torpedoes. One minute later, Walker ordered his ships to open up with their 5in guns.

Ijuin's maneuvers had placed his four ships to the southwest of the Americans with all four destroyers steaming on a parallel course in echelon. The closest ship, *Yugumo*, was only 3,300yd from Walker's lead ship. She became the target of the gunnery from all three American ships, and immediately executed a quick turn to launch all eight of her ready torpedoes at the Americans at 2256hrs. Two minutes later, *Yugumo* was struck by at least five shells. She lost steering control and was unable to follow the rest of Ijuin's group, which turned to starboard to present their sterns to any American torpedoes in the water and made smoke.

One of *Yugumo*'s torpedoes struck *Chevalier*, which destroyed the bow forward of the bridge. Walker continued to the northwest to engage Hara's two ships, which were trailing some 5 miles behind Ijuin's group. Led by *Shigure*, Hara's two ships turned to the northwest at 2259hrs and planned a deliberate torpedo attack on the Americans now steaming on a parallel course. Again, in the words of Hara:

> Seeing the enemy column take a right turn, I ordered another hard right at 2058 [The Japanese used Tokyo time, thus accounting for the difference]. We were 8,500 meters [9,296yd] from our intended targets. My running ahead discouraged the enemy from attacking with torpedoes, and permitted me to choose my own time and angle for launching at him.
>
> We ran some 500 meters [547yd] in closing the American force before I ordered a left turn and release of torpedoes. The enemy was 50 degrees to starboard, an ideal torpedo angle, and distance 7,500 meters [8,202yd]. Sixteen fish shooshed into the water from my two ships, and torpedomen immediately began to reload the tubes. (Hara n.d.: 210)

One of these found *Selfridge* at 2306hrs, and blew the bow of the ship off. Just before the arrival of the Japanese torpedoes, *O'Bannon* had collided with the crippled *Chevalier*, which was unseen through all the smoke of the flashless powder.

Ijuin did not grasp the opportunity to finish off the American force now in complete disarray. At 2313hrs, Japanese aircraft spotted the second American destroyer division coming from the east. Thinking these were the cruisers he had been warned about, he changed course to the northwest and continued out of the area. At 2317hrs, he fired a full 24-torpedo salvo at the two American cripples now located some 16,000yd away. None hit. Hara's two ships followed behind, and the brief battle was over.

Three ships were left crippled at the conclusion of the action. *Yugumo* was the first to go. At 2305hrs, she was probably hit by one of the five torpedoes launched from *Chevalier* as the crew jettisoned all excess weight in an attempt to save their ship. *Yugumo* sank minutes later, and only 25 of her crew were saved by using an American lifeboat left in the area. The next day, another 78 were picked up by American PT boats. *Chevalier* could not be saved, and was scuttled by a torpedo the next day; 54 of her crew were lost. Another 49 were killed aboard *Selfridge* but the ship was saved and returned to service seven months later. *O'Bannon* also reached port and suffered no casualties.

This faded March 28, 1942 shot of *Kazegumo* shows her on the day she was commissioned. This unit of the Yugumo class participated in the battle of Vella Lavella. She was later sunk by submarine attack in June 1944. (Yamato Museum)

THE BATTLE OF CAPE ST. GEORGE

The final destroyer clash of the Solomons campaign came almost two months later. It was proof that the US Navy had fully digested the lessons begun in August 1942 and that it had finally learned to best the IJN at night.

On November 1, Wilkinson landed the 3rd Marine Division at Cape Torokina located to the north of Empress Augusta Bay on Bougainville. This was the last island before New Britain where Rabaul was located, which prompted the Japanese to make a major effort to repel the landing. The Japanese committed *Sentai* 5 (Squadron 5 composed of heavy cruisers) as well as Destroyer Squadron 10 and what remained of Ijuin's Destroyer Squadron 3. Facing them were the four light cruisers and eight destroyers of Merrill's Task Force 39. Included in the American force were the four Fletcher-class destroyers of Burke's Destroyer Division 45. On November 2, Merrill's force intercepted the Japanese and instigated the battle of Empress Augusta Bay. Merrill had determined to use Burke's new tactics and intended to let his destroyers attack first, and only open fire with his cruisers after the torpedoes had done their damage. Most importantly, he planned to keep his cruisers at ranges between 16,000 and 20,000yd and to change course frequently; this made him the first cruiser commander to respect the threat of the Type 93 torpedo.

This is destroyer *Selfridge* after the battle of Vella Lavella. A single Type 93 torpedo blew off her bow as far back as the No. 2 twin 5in mount. Alongside her is *O'Bannon*, which was damaged by collision during the action. (NHHC 80-G-274873)

Fletcher-class unit *Chevalier* had a brief but busy combat career. She arrived in the South Pacific in January 1943, and in May 1943 covered minelaying operations in the Blackett Strait and Kula Gulf that cost the Japanese three destroyers. She also participated in bombardments of Kolombangara and New Georgia during May and July. Damaged on July 5 while helping to rescue the crew of the torpedoed destroyer *Strong*, she was under repair for much of the rest of that month. *Chevalier* next took part in the battle off Horaniu on August 18. At the battle of Vella Lavella, she was hit by a single Type 93 torpedo and had her bow blown off as far aft as the bridge. She was further damaged amidships by a collision with *O'Bannon*. After her surviving crewmen had been removed, *Chevalier* was scuttled by a torpedo from destroyer *La Vallette*. (NHHC 80-G-43647)

The battle did not play out as either side intended. After Burke's torpedo attack proved ineffective due to a Japanese course change, Merrill opened fire with his cruisers. The target was light cruiser *Sendai*, which was quickly hit and crippled. She later sank, as did a destroyer damaged in a collision with one of the Japanese heavy cruisers. Japanese torpedoes struck a destroyer but she was saved. The Americans had successfully repelled a major Japanese operation in a night engagement with minimal losses.

Following the battle of Empress Augusta Bay, the Japanese resumed night reinforcement destroyer runs. To conduct a reinforcement mission to Buka Island located north of Bougainville, the Japanese planned to use three destroyers to move personnel and then evacuate unemployed aviation personnel. The three transport destroyers were covered by two other destroyers. The three transport destroyers arrived at Buka late on November 24 and quickly loaded their passengers and departed at 0045hrs on the 25th.

The battle of Cape St. George, November 25, 1943
American forces
Destroyer Squadron 23 (Captain Arleigh A. Burke on *Charles Ausburne*)
Destroyer Division 45 (Captain Burke): *Charles Ausburne* (Fletcher class); *Claxton* (Fletcher class); *Dyson* (Fletcher class)
Destroyer Division 46 (Commander B. Austin on *Spence*): *Converse* (Fletcher class); *Spence* (Fletcher class)
Japanese forces
Support Force (Captain Kagawa Kiyoto on *Onami*): *Onami* (Yugumo class); *Makinami* (Yugumo class)
Transport Group (Captain Yamashiro Katsumori on *Amagiri*): *Amagiri* (Fubuki class); *Yugiri* (Fubuki class); *Uzuki* (Mutsuki class)

The Americans had prior notice that a transport operation was planned from Rabaul and Halsey sent Burke's Destroyer Squadron 23 to oppose it. When the Japanese departed Buka, Burke's destroyers were waiting. Visibility was poor with no moon, so Japanese lookouts were outperformed on this occasion by American electronics. At

0141hrs, the radar aboard *Dyson* gained first contact on the two screening Japanese destroyers at 22,000yd. Burke turned to the east to close the Japanese. Burke waited until 0156hrs when the Japanese were only 5,500yd away to launch his torpedoes. Each ship fired five torpedoes and immediately made a turn to the south to avoid the expected Japanese counterattack.

On board *Onami*, lookouts had spotted retiring shadows to the west, but before the Japanese could react, the American torpedoes shattered Kagawa's force. Several torpedoes hit *Onami* and she sank quickly leaving no survivors. Another torpedo hit the trailing *Makinami*, but she remained afloat.

After launching his torpedoes, the American radar gained contact on the Japanese transport group some 13,000yd to the northeast. Burke took off to the north to engage the fleeing Japanese. After realizing the fate of the support group, the Japanese commander headed north to clear the area. Burke pursued at full speed, 33kts,

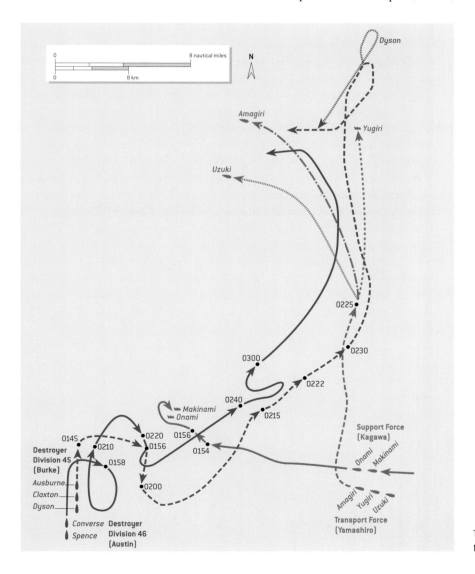

The battle of Cape St. George, November 25, 1943.

engaging the Japanese with the two forward 5in mounts of his destroyers. *Yugiri* fired three torpedoes at the American column, but they missed after Burke executed a well-timed evasion maneuver. In Burke's own words, the maneuver could have meant the difference between victory and defeat:

> No sooner had the … division come to course … than three heavy explosions were felt by all ships. The explosions were so heavy the ships were badly jarred and the Squadron Commander could not resist the temptation to look at the bow to see whether or not it was still there. *Charles Ausburne* did not slow, and it was felt that at least one of the ships astern had been hit by torpedoes. Each one of the ships astern thought that one of the other ships had been hit. Fortunately the explosions were merely Japanese torpedoes exploding at the end of their runs or as they crossed our wakes. It may be that the short jog to the right threw the division out of torpedo water. If so, it was one of the most fortunate of the many lucky breaks the squadron experienced. (Roscoe 1966: 266)

At 0225hrs, the Japanese commander split his force, with each of his ships going in a different direction. The largest radar return was *Yugiri* as she headed north, and Burke decided to take all three of his ships to chase her.

American gunnery continued to hit *Yugiri*, and within 30 minutes they had closed the range to 8,800yd. A hit at 0305hrs on *Yugiri*'s engineering spaces further reduced her speed. This forced her captain to come about to face her tormentors, launching all her remaining torpedoes and engaging with her guns. All three American destroyers engaged the defiant *Yugiri* with guns and torpedoes. She sank at 0328hrs, only 60 miles east of Cape St. George on the island of New Ireland. However, later that day a Japanese submarine saved 278 of the destroyers' crews and the aviation personnel.

Austin's two destroyers were ordered to finish off the crippled *Makinami* after Burke took off to chase the fleeing transport group. *Converse* engaged the *Makinami* with five torpedoes and claimed two hits. At 0228hrs, Austin followed up with a gunnery attack, but the Japanese destroyer did not sink until 0254hrs following four major explosions of her magazines. Only 28 of her crew survived. The other two Japanese destroyers reached Rabaul. Burke had capped the Solomons campaign with an outstanding victory. For no loss to himself, he had sunk three Japanese destroyers in a textbook action.

LEFT Burke and Rear Admiral Merrill (right center) formed an effective team during the Solomons campaign. Here, Burke introduces Merrill to the crews of *Charles Ausburne* and *Claxton* during an awards ceremony held on board *Charles Ausburne* in Purvis Bay, Florida Island, Solomon Islands, on January 30, 1944. (NHHC 80-G-214936)

RIGHT *Charles Ausburne* receiving mail by highline from light cruiser *Columbia* while steaming in the Solomon Islands on September 27, 1943. *Charles Ausburne* participated in several actions off Vella Lavella and the battles of Empress Augusta Bay and Cape St. George. (NHHC 80-G-201993)

STATISTICS AND ANALYSIS

The series of battles fought in the Central and Northern Solomons between March and November 1943 were the last in the process that began in August 1942 and which gutted the IJN's destroyer force. Of the seven battles fought after March 1943, three involved Allied cruiser–destroyer forces and four were strictly destroyer duels.

After a rough start in July 1943, the Americans hit their stride. From August through November 1943, the American sank nine Japanese ships in surface engagements in the Solomons, six by torpedo. In exchange, the Japanese sank a single American destroyer. This was a remarkable change compared to the results of the night battles off Guadalcanal in 1942 in which American surface forces sank a total of seven Japanese ships, all by gunfire, while losing 15 ships to Japanese surface forces, ten of which were sunk by Type 93 torpedoes.

A closer examination of each of the destroyer battles traces the improvements in the fortunes of the US Navy. The battle of Vella Gulf was a total victory for the Americans. Moosbrugger had a solid plan and used his weapons flawlessly. He took advantage of local conditions to exploit his advantage in radar. This marked the first time in the war that Japanese destroyers had been beaten in a night action. It was also the first time in the Solomons campaign that American destroyers had independently engaged the Japanese. The results of the new doctrine and reliance on torpedo tactics were immediate and dramatic.

The engagement cost the Japanese three destroyers sunk. Of their crews and passengers, 1,210 aboard died and only 310 survived. The reason for the Japanese defeat was simple – they had been taken totally by surprise. On this occasion, their

After the three Japanese
destroyers of the Transport
Group landed their troops and
loaded 700 aviation personnel at
Buka, they left the harbor at
0045hrs and headed west for
Rabaul. Outside the harbor they
joined with the two destroyers of
the Support Group. Yugumo-class
destroyer *Onami* was at the head
of the Japanese formation. The
night was very dark with no
moon. Visibility was only about
3,000yd by visual means and
this was reduced by frequent
rain squalls in the area. The
American destroyer radars
picked up the Japanese force at
22,000yd at 0141hrs and turned
to the east to launch an attack.
At 0156hrs, the Japanese were
only 5,500yd away and Burke
decided to launch his torpedoes
at the unsuspecting Japanese
with each of his three ships firing
five weapons. Immediately after
the launch, Burke ordered his
ships to turn 90 degrees and
head away from the Japanese at
30kts to avoid a counter-strike.
After three and a half minutes,
the American torpedoes found
their targets with devastating
results. As shown in this scene,
at least two torpedoes struck
Onami, which created massive
explosions and a 300ft fireball.
The Japanese were totally
surprised with their weapons still
trained fore and aft. At 0159hrs,
lookouts on *Onami* had spotted
the shadows of the retreating
American destroyers, but there
was no time to react. *Onami* blew
up with all hands, including the
commander of Destroyer
Squadron 31, Captain Kagawa
Kiyoto, and the ship's captain,
Commander Kikkawa Kiyoshi. He
was posthumously promoted
two ranks, the only IJN destroyer
skipper so honored during the
war.

lookouts had failed to spot the Americans in time. The result was disaster. If they had gained only a few extra minutes, the result could have been very different.

In the next destroyer action, off Horaniu, the result was an inconclusive draw. When they lost surprise, the American had no chance of repeating their success at Vella Gulf. The usual Japanese torpedo tactics were ineffective when the Americans executed well-timed maneuvers taking them out of torpedo danger. Despite their confidence in radar-controlled gunnery, the Americans succeeded in only slightly damaging two Japanese destroyers with the expenditure of 3,028 5in rounds. Admiral Ijuin accomplished his mission of getting the convoy through to Vella Lavella, but had inflicted no damage on the Americans.

At the battle of Vella Lavella, the Japanese gained a tactical victory since they inflicted more damage on the Americans than they suffered and accomplished their mission of evacuating the garrison on Vella Lavella. However, trading one Japanese destroyer for one American destroyer sunk was not a recipe for the long-term success of the IJN. Ijuin had wasted a chance to inflict a sharp local defeat on the Americans by not taking his five intact destroyers to finish off the shattered American formation.

The American performance at Vella Lavella was uneven. If nothing else, Walker showed extreme aggressiveness, but at the cost of having his entire force damaged or destroyed. His biggest mistake was not to order his force to change course after launching his torpedoes, thus making his force vulnerable to counterattack. Walker claimed three destroyers sunk and several others damaged, but in reality had sunk only a single Japanese destroyer.

Burke's victory at Cape St. George was the best example to date of the US Navy's winning combination of aggressive leadership, superior technology, and well-aimed torpedoes. His victory was the result of a well-planned and executed surprise torpedo attack. It also showed that the margin for victory was thin. Had the two Japanese torpedo attacks not narrowly missed their intended targets, the result would have been different.

As bad as the results of the March–November 1943 battles were for the Japanese, they do not even tell the full extent of Japanese losses. In total, 25 destroyers were lost during 1943 in the Solomons or in the Bismarck Sea. Added to the 11 destroyers already lost off Guadalcanal, these were severe losses that were impossible to replace.

Put in simple terms, at the start of the Solomons campaign in August 1942, the IJN was the hunter and the US Navy the hunted. This was especially true in night engagements where the IJN began the campaign with superior numbers, weapons, and tactics. Even after their losses in the Guadalcanal battles, these Japanese advantages persisted into 1943. However, even when they were generally successful, the rising toll of attrition was beginning to be too much for the IJN to bear.

By mid-1943, the Americans had the required building blocks in place for victory. With a new collection of aggressive and battle-tested leadership in place, combined with new tactics, the result was a dramatic turn-around from the night battles of 1942. Overarching this was the continuing American edge in technology. Increasingly, the Americans were more comfortable with the advantages offered by radar and molded their tactics to take full benefit of this priceless advantage. While Japanese optics were often able to negate the advantage of radar, this became rarer in the battles fought later in 1943. In a night engagement, the element of surprise was key. This was shown by

Converse, a Fletcher-class destroyer, is pictured in the South Pacific in March 1944. As a member of Burke's Destroyer Squadron 23, she participated in the battle of Cape St. George. She ended her career in the Spanish Navy after World War II. (NHHC 80-G-232120)

the fact that the two victories gained by American destroyers in 1943 were the result of a surprise torpedo attack set up by radar. In the other two battles where surprise was lost, the Japanese were able to gain a victory or a draw. Dominance over the IJN was gained when the Americans learned to fully employ radar and to employ both gunnery and torpedoes. When scratch task forces were assembled to go after the Japanese with ineffective doctrine, the results were predictable. In these battles, the Americans relied on gunnery and aggressive action to carry the day. Once a more effective doctrine that combined guns and torpedoes was fully integrated, the Japanese suffered increasingly heavy losses and inflicted little damage in return.

AFTERMATH

After the battle of Cape St. George, there were no further major destroyer clashes between the Americans and Japanese. The Japanese destroyer force never played an important role in any future Pacific battle. The Solomons campaign had crippled the force, and added to future heavy losses at the hands of American aircraft and especially submarines, the Japanese were continually challenged to even provide suitable destroyer escort for major fleet operations. As an example, for the invasion of the Marianas in June 1944, the US Navy was able to provide some 62 destroyers for the carrier task force alone, while the Japanese only mustered 27. The weakness of the Japanese destroyer screen was amply shown when American submarines torpedoed two Japanese carriers during the battle.

In spite of their impressive showing against American surface units in the Solomons, the fact that Japanese destroyers were maximized for surface warfare and were fairly ineffective in other warfare areas was clearly shown during the second part of the war. Pounded by American air power and hounded by American submarines, the Japanese lost a total of 40 fleet destroyers in 1944. In October 1944 at the battle of Leyte Gulf, 11 Japanese destroyers were presented with another chance to deal a serious blow to an outnumbered and outgunned American force off Samar. Facing only three American destroyers, the Japanese destroyers acted in a timid manner and did not close for a torpedo attack. A full barrage of Type 93 torpedoes resulted in no hits.

By the time that the IJN made its last major sortie in April 1945 to attack the American invasion force off Okinawa, only eight destroyers remained operational to accompany superbattleship *Yamato* on her final voyage.

The American destroyer force achieved even greater success in 1944 than it did in the last battles of the Solomons campaign. Taking aggressive action to a new level, and employing tactics designed to maximize their torpedo capabilities, American destroyers

Yugiri, shown here in 1930, was a member of Group II of the Special Type destroyer class. The ten units of Group II differed in several respects from those of Group I, principally with regard to the Type B 5in gun mounts, a modified and enlarged bridge structure, and different types of stacks and ventilation. *Yugiri* was sunk by gunfire at the battle of Cape St. George in November 1943. (Yamato Museum)

achieved several signal successes in the series of encounters known collectively as the battle of Leyte Gulf. In the battle of Surigao Strait on October 25, 1944, the Americans laid a trap for a Japanese force of two battleships, one heavy cruiser, and four destroyers. Destroyers were deployed well in advance of the American battle line, and their well-executed torpedo assault hit both battleships (sinking one) and three of the destroyers. Later that same day, in the battle of Samar, a force of three American destroyers and four destroyer escorts faced a Japanese force of four battleships, six heavy and two light cruisers, and 11 destroyers. The American destroyers, aided by the aircraft of the escort carriers they were assigned to protect, simply outfought the Japanese and managed to torpedo a heavy cruiser. This epic action cost the Americans two destroyers and a destroyer escort sunk, but served as an eternal testimony to the courage and skill of American destroyermen.

Japanese Type 93 torpedoes accounted for one more American destroyer when on December 3, 1944 a Japanese destroyer escort sank a Sumner-class (an enlarged version of the Fletcher class) ship with a single torpedo in Ormoc Bay off the island of Leyte. The sternest test of the war for American destroyers was not against Japanese surface forces, but against Japanese air attacks, including extensive kamikaze operations, while operating off Okinawa from April until June 1945. Though 13 destroyers were sunk and many others damaged by kamikaze, some beyond repair, American destroyers proved versatile enough to survive this threat as well. When the US Navy entered Tokyo Bay to accept the Japanese surrender in September 1945, destroyers were in the lead.

BIBLIOGRAPHY

Campbell, John (2002). *Naval Weapons of World War Two*. Greenwich: Conway Maritime Press.

Cracknell, William H. (1971). "USS Charles Ausburne" in *Warships in Profile 1*. Windsor: Profile Publications Ltd.

Crenshaw, Russell Sydnor, Jr. (1998). *South Pacific Destroyer*. Annapolis, MD: Naval Institute Press.

Dull, Paul (1978). *A Battle History of the Imperial Japanese Navy (1941–1945)*. Annapolis, MD: Naval Institute Press.

Evans, David C. & Mark R. Peattie (1997). *Kaigun*. Annapolis, MD: Naval Institute Press.

Friedman, Norman (1981). *Naval Radar*. Greenwich: Conway Maritime Press.

Friedman, Norman (2004). *U.S. Destroyers*. Annapolis, MD: Naval Institute Press.

Friedman, Norman (2008). *Naval Firepower*. Annapolis, MD: Naval Institute Press.

Hara, Tameichi (n.d.). *Japanese Destroyer Captain*. Annapolis, MD: Naval Institute Press. Originally published in Japan as *Teikoku Kaigun No Saigo* in 1958.

Hodges, Peter & Norman Friedman (1979). *Destroyer Weapons of World War 2*. Greenwich: Conway Maritime Press.

Hone, Trent (2006). "'Give Them Hell!': The US Navy's Night Combat Doctrine and the Campaign for Guadalcanal," *War in History* 13(2), 171–99.

Itani, Jiro, Hans Lengerer, & Tomoko Rehm-Takahara (1991). "Japanese Oxygen Torpedoes and Fire Control Systems," *Warship 1991*. Greenwich: Conway Maritime Press.

Marder, Arthur J. (1981). *Old Friends, New Enemies*. Oxford: Clarendon Press.

O'Hara, Vincent P. (2007). *The US Navy Against the Axis*. Annapolis, MD: Naval Institute Press.

Yudachi, shown here in 1936 shortly before commissioning, was a member of the Shiratsuyu class. These were essentially repeats of the modified Hatsuhara class, and retained the same basic layout and armament. *Yudachi* was sunk by gunfire during the First Naval Battle of Guadalcanal in November 1942. (Yamato Museum)

Preston, Anthony, ed. (1978). *Super Destroyers*. Greenwich: Conway Maritime Press.

Reardon, Jeff (2011). "Breaking the US Navy's 'Gun Club' Mentality in the South Pacific," *The Journal of Military History* 75, April 2011, 533–64.

Reilly, John C., Jr. (1983). *United States Navy Destroyers of World War II*. Poole: Blandford Press.

Roscoe, Theodore (1966). *United States Destroyer Operations in World War II*. Annapolis, MD: Naval Institute Press.

Stern, Robert C. (2008). *Destroyer Battles*. Annapolis, MD: Naval Institute Press.

Watts, A.J. & B.G. Gordon (1971). *The Imperial Japanese Navy*. London: MacDonald & Company.

Whitley, M.J. (1988). *Destroyers of World War Two*. Annapolis, MD: Naval Institute Press.

Wildenberg, Thomas & Norman Polmar (2010). *Ship Killer*. Annapolis, MD: Naval Institute Press.

A fine beam view of Yugumo-class unit *Makigumo* in March 1942. The Yugumo class was very similar to the preceding Kagero class with the primary exception of introducing the Type D 5in gun mount and a streamlined bridge structure. *Makigumo* was sunk February 1, 1943 after hitting a mine trying to avoid a PT-boat attack during the evacuation of Guadalcanal. (Yamato Museum)

INDEX

References to illustrations are shown in **bold**